SO YOU CALL YOURSELF A CHRISTIAN?

Personal Responsibility
Kingdom Within
Unconditional LOVE
Perfection
Oneness

BY

BENNY R. FERGUSON JR.

So You Call Yourself A Christian?

So You Call Yourself A Christian?
© 2018 by Benny R. Ferguson Jr.
All rights reserved

ISBN:

Published by:

The Ferguson Company

Editing: Ari's Editing House
http://roxanec.wix.com/time-to-read.com

2

Benny Ferguson

Dear Reader,

In the establishing of this work, it has been fascinating to see that teachings that I thought I may have to abandon because of new understandings about life that were proving themselves true to me, were actually directly in line with the teachings from where I began my journey. As it is true that everyone's journey is different, and that it is highly unlikely that any one teaching will reveal all of the secrets of life to you, it is true that the path to understanding is a universal path, and that is the path of LOVE.

The teachings of Jesus are not the teachings of a figure whose goal was to create a religious movement that would attract and convert followers, with its many complexities, rules, and rituals. The teachings of Jesus, simply put, set down the "Way of Life" necessary to allow alignment of thoughts, feelings, words, and deeds with the Source of all that is. Whatever name you have for the Source—the essence of life, from which all things material and nonmaterial emanate—is irrelevant.

This "Way of Life", is a personal path that is not restricted to one religious sect, but is open to all as a marked way into the Kingdom of Heaven, a life of health, wealth, abundance and beauty. This was the wish of Jesus, that his fellow human beings might be reminded that LOVE is the ultimate power, and that its presence in the life of the individual reveals the face of God to the world. Yet, it befalls us to choose to walk the path of LOVE. We must ultimately grow the faith to realize our own magnificence.

I invite the reader, no matter what faith you ascribe to, to open your minds for a moment, and see the true message of Jesus. A message of personal responsibility, a message of power, a description of the "Way of Life" that reveals our true nature and our true potential, as it pertains to this physical life.

Benny R. Ferguson Jr.
October 2010

3

So You Call Yourself A Christian?

Introduction

In a global society where changes are constant and where those things that are permanent and can be trusted to stand are few to none, there is a way to find peace. This peace, this place is far from where most think it is, and closer than many will ever realize. The destination, which most do not realize they are looking for, resides deep within each and every one of us. For those who believe in God—the Source of all creation—and for those who do not believe in God, there is a universal answer to their lives, pain and suffering that it currently entails. This, my friends, is your inner most being.

Within the twists and turns that flow through the eternity of that which we call time, there have been those who have lived and walked among us who have proclaimed to know the way, a way out of pain and suffering. A way to the realization of truth, and Christ Jesus was such a guide. This book is going to delve deeply into uncharted territory. For those who claim Christianity as their chosen way to peace, to salvation, this book is going to challenge what they think they know. It is going to bring briefly and directly to your attention what has always been before you, what has always been there, but obviously have omitted to notice. This book is going to make you ask, "Is my life a reflection of God's strength, glory and power, or have I mistaken it for weakness, pain and suffering?" The courage to look and truly see resides within you, but you must look and ask the right questions, the challenging questions, because if God is the Father, the Source of all, then your questions are welcome, as the questions from a child to its physical father would be.

Who are you in relation to God the Source, and Jesus? Why are you here? Are you here just to suffer and flounder in your feeble attempt to accomplish something, things that are far cries, laughing matters, when it comes to the dreams and inspirations that well up in you occasionally, but that you dismiss because you do not believe they can happen or do not see how they can be possible for you. If your current beliefs do not show you the way, if they do not assist you in clearing the path to understanding and knowing that everything you have ever been inspired to do, you could and can accomplish, then they are holding you back or down. Take your pick.

What was Jesus really saying? Did he come to start a movement (Christianity), with its traditions and rituals, or did he teach a way of life? Did he come to tell us all that we are now his servants, or was there a lot more to it?

Jesus is the greatest figure in the bible, yet the most misunderstood. This is because his teachings are the most misquoted. The true meanings of "Jesus' Teachings" have been masked by confusion and attempts at control for so long that the words, which actually lie on the pages, are not even seen.

It is time to lift the curtain draped over our minds. It is time to separate ourselves from the confusion and disbelief that has been present since the disciples walked with Jesus himself.

Do you feel strength growing inside with your current understanding, or are you stagnant? Do you see yourself ever having dominion over your life, or are you stuck thanking a God who laughs at all of your hard times and throws you a line, a miracle every now and then?

I challenge you to read the following pages with an open mind and an open heart. I challenge you to evaluate your current understanding of "The Man" himself, as we look at his words, no one else's, and ask, "What did he say?" and "Was he talking to me?"

LOVE

Chapter I

What Do You Mean I Am Responsible?

In the following scriptures, we are looking for the characteristics of the person that is allowing God to work in and through them. This type of person is allowing and drawing the rewards of the "Kingdom of God".

We are also looking for whether these characteristics are given to a special type of person, or if it is each individual's responsibility to grow and develop these characteristics in themselves.

✓ **Qualities**

Matthew 5:3-10

Are you humbly and earnestly seeking God, the Source of all Creation?

3 Blessed are the poor in spirit: for theirs is the kingdom of heaven.

4 Blessed are they that mourn: for they shall be comforted.

5 Blessed are the meek: for they shall inherit the earth.

6 Blessed are they which do hunger and thirst after righteousness: for they shall be filled.

7 Blessed are the merciful: for they shall obtain mercy.

8 Blessed are the pure in heart: for they shall see God.

⁹ Blessed are the peacemakers: for they shall be called the children of God.

¹⁰Blessed are they which are persecuted for righteousness' sake: for theirs is the kingdom of heaven.

Matthew 5:13-14

Are you the Source of Purity and Love for all that come in contact with you?

¹³Ye are the salt of the earth: but if the salt have lost his savour, wherewith shall it be salted? it is thenceforth good for nothing, but to be cast out, and to be trodden under foot of men.

¹⁴Ye are the light of the world. A city that is set on an hill cannot be hid.

Matthew 5:22-25

Do you truly let go and forgive yourself and others? If not you are not forgiven.

²²But I say unto you, That whosoever is angry with his brother without a cause shall be in danger of the judgment: and whosoever shall say to his brother, Raca, shall be in danger of the council: but whosoever shall say, Thou fool, shall be in danger of hell fire.

²³Therefore if thou bring thy gift to the altar, and there rememberest that thy brother hath ought against thee;

²⁴Leave there thy gift before the altar, and go thy way; first be reconciled to thy brother, and then come and offer thy gift.

²⁵Agree with thine adversary quickly, whiles thou art in the way with him; lest at any time the adversary deliver thee to the

judge, and the judge deliver thee to the officer, and thou be cast into prison.

Matthew 5:37

Are you decisive or do you have to think about it?

37But let your communication be, Yea, yea; Nay, nay: for whatsoever is more than these cometh of evil.

Matthew 6:1-4

Do you do good deeds because you are led to, or do you only seek recognition?

¹ Take heed that ye do not your alms before men, to be seen of them: otherwise ye have no reward of your Father which is in heaven.

² Therefore when thou doest thine alms, do not sound a trumpet before thee, as the hypocrites do in the synagogues and in the streets, that they may have glory of men. Verily I say unto you, They have their reward.

³ But when thou doest alms, let not thy left hand know what thy right hand doeth:

⁴ That thine alms may be in secret: and thy Father which seeth in secret himself shall reward thee openly.

Matthew 6:14-15

Do you truly forgive?

14For if ye forgive men their trespasses, your heavenly Father will also forgive you:

15But if ye forgive not men their trespasses, neither will your Father forgive your trespasses.

So You Call Yourself A Christian?

Matthew 6:25-34

Do you truly have faith that you will be taken care of and provided for?

[25]Therefore I say unto you, Take no thought for your life, what ye shall eat, or what ye shall drink; nor yet for your body, what ye shall put on. Is not the life more than meat, and the body than raiment?

[26]Behold the fowls of the air: for they sow not, neither do they reap, nor gather into barns; yet your heavenly Father feedeth them. Are ye not much better than they?

[27]Which of you by taking thought can add one cubit unto his stature?

[28]And why take ye thought for raiment? Consider the lilies of the field, how they grow; they toil not, neither do they spin:

[29]And yet I say unto you, That even Solomon in all his glory was not arrayed like one of these.

[30]Wherefore, if God so clothe the grass of the field, which to day is, and to morrow is cast into the oven, shall he not much more clothe you, O ye of little faith?

[31]Therefore take no thought, saying, What shall we eat? or, What shall we drink? or, Wherewithal shall we be clothed?

[32](For after all these things do the Gentiles seek:) for your heavenly Father knoweth that ye have need of all these things.

[33]But seek ye first the kingdom of God, and his righteousness; and all these things shall be added unto you.

[34]Take therefore no thought for the morrow: for the morrow shall take thought for the things of itself. Sufficient unto the day is the evil thereof.

Benny Ferguson

Matthew 7:1-5

The type of person you are, is bestowed upon you 100%.

¹ Judge not, that ye be not judged.

² For with what judgment ye judge, ye shall be judged: and with what measure ye mete, it shall be measured to you again.

³ And why beholdest thou the mote that is in thy brother's eye, but considerest not the beam that is in thine own eye?

⁴ Or how wilt thou say to thy brother, Let me pull out the mote out of thine eye; and, behold, a beam is in thine own eye?

⁵ Thou hypocrite, first cast out the beam out of thine own eye; and then shalt thou see clearly to cast out the mote out of thy brother's eye.

Matthew 18:1-5

Are you fully open, empty of mind and heart?

¹ At the same time came the disciples unto Jesus, saying, Who is the greatest in the kingdom of heaven?

² And Jesus called a little child unto him, and set him in the midst of them,

³ And said, Verily I say unto you, Except ye be converted, and become as little children, ye shall not enter into the kingdom of heaven.

⁴ Whosoever therefore shall humble himself as this little child, the same is greatest in the kingdom of heaven.

⁵ And whoso shall receive one such little child in my name receiveth me.

Matthew 18:15

15Moreover if thy brother shall trespass against thee, go and tell him his fault between thee and him alone: if he shall hear thee, thou hast gained thy brother.

Matthew 18:23-35

The Kingdom returns that which you are and do 100%.

23Therefore is the kingdom of heaven likened unto a certain king, which would take account of his servants.

24And when he had begun to reckon, one was brought unto him, which owed him ten thousand talents.

25But forasmuch as he had not to pay, his lord commanded him to be sold, and his wife, and children, and all that he had, and payment to be made.

26The servant therefore fell down, and worshipped him, saying, Lord, have patience with me, and I will pay thee all.

27Then the lord of that servant was moved with compassion, and loosed him, and forgave him the debt.

28But the same servant went out, and found one of his fellowservants, which owed him an hundred pence: and he laid hands on him, and took him by the throat, saying, Pay me that thou owest.

29And his fellowservant fell down at his feet, and besought him, saying, Have patience with me, and I will pay thee all.

30And he would not: but went and cast him into prison, till he should pay the debt.

31So when his fellowservants saw what was done, they were very sorry, and came and told unto their lord all that was done.

32Then his lord, after that he had called him, said unto him, O thou wicked servant, I forgave thee all that debt, because thou desiredst me:

33Shouldest not thou also have had compassion on thy fellowservant, even as I had pity on thee?

34And his lord was wroth, and delivered him to the tormentors, till he should pay all that was due unto him.

35So likewise shall my heavenly Father do also unto you, if ye from your hearts forgive not every one his brother their trespasses.

Mark 9:35

If you wish to be first, you must provide the greatest service.

35And he sat down, and called the twelve, and saith unto them, If any man desire to be first, the same shall be last of all, and servant of all.

Luke 11:34-36

What is your focus?

34The light of the body is the eye: therefore when thine eye is single, thy whole body also is full of light; but when thine eye is evil, thy body also is full of darkness.

35Take heed therefore that the light which is in thee be not darkness.

36If thy whole body therefore be full of light, having no part dark, the whole shall be full of light, as when the bright shining of a candle doth give thee light.

13

So You Call Yourself A Christian?

Luke 14:7-11

Are you humble?

7 And he put forth a parable to those which were bidden, when he marked how they chose out the chief rooms; saying unto them.

8 When thou art bidden of any man to a wedding, sit not down in the highest room; lest a more honourable man than thou be bidden of him;

9 And he that bade thee and him come and say to thee, Give this man place; and thou begin with shame to take the lowest room.

10But when thou art bidden, go and sit down in the lowest room; that when he that bade thee cometh, he may say unto thee, Friend, go up higher: then shalt thou have worship in the presence of them that sit at meat with thee.

11For whosoever exalteth himself shall be abased; and he that humbleth himself shall be exalted.

Luke 14:13-14

Are you a blessing without seeking reward or appreciation?

13But when thou makest a feast, call the poor, the maimed, the lame, the blind:

14And thou shalt be blessed; for they cannot recompense thee: for thou shalt be recompensed at the resurrection of the just.

Luke 16:13

Are you following and growing in the Light or not?

¹³No servant can serve two masters: for either he will hate the one, and love the other; or else he will hold to the one, and despise the other. Ye cannot serve God and mammon.

The qualities of that individual, that person, that human being who is actively engaged in the recreation of himself through the "Teachings of Christ Jesus", are actually few but powerful, and when looked at, their Truth can and will be noticed in individuals you come in contact with, who are unknowingly exuding them. First of the key qualities is Humbleness. This is humbleness to God, not to man. The Humbleness that you have in and to God the Source is in reverence for the infinite knowledge, strength, energy, and power to which you have access as long as you stay connected to the Source of your being. For when connected, you do not seek or need recognition, acceptance, or approval from your physical brothers or sisters; you are comfortable within yourself to move forward in all that you know is right and spirit-led. Focus is another great quality of one who is actively engaged in the practice of the "Teachings of Jesus". This focus can be likened to children who are set or fixed on something they want no matter what. You have repeatedly asked them to "Stop," or told them "No," and they absolutely do not hear you. This is the focus required of you. It is a focus on God, God's Love, God's Words and God's actions, so that all you do might be in alignment with God. When it is not, you will know it, and you will recognize that it is an area for growth which needs your attention. All of the qualities mentioned in the scriptures are needed to allow God's presence to grow and be made manifest in your innermost being and in your life. Of these qualities, however, focus on God is the greatest. This focus will grow in you in the likeness of God. The right qualities, the right attitudes, and the right demeanors will begin to set in and become your normal, natural state of being. You will realize then that all you thought you needed to be, you were already; you just weren't recognizing it. The focus on God the Source will compel you to learn about, and realize your true self. It will compel you to begin the process of removing all of the habits, attitudes, and ways of thinking, speaking, and acting, which have burdened your true being for so long. You will realize then and ultimately, that these things do not truly line up with the character and will of God the Source.

✓ **Thy Faith**

In this section we are looking for whether God's power was merely displayed by Jesus, or if it was released unto and through each individual, on an individual basis, and why Jesus was not able to do mighty works in his own land even though he desired to do so.

Matthew 9:2

2 And, behold, they brought to him a man sick of the palsy, lying on a bed: and Jesus seeing their faith said unto the sick of the palsy; Son, be of good cheer; thy sins be forgiven thee.

Matthew 9:22

22But Jesus turned him about, and when he saw her, he said, Daughter, be of good comfort; thy faith hath made thee whole. And the woman was made whole from that hour.

Matthew 9:28-29

28And when he was come into the house, the blind men came to him: and Jesus saith unto them, Believe ye that I am able to do this? They said unto him, Yea, Lord.

29Then touched he their eyes, saying, According to your faith be it unto you.

Matthew 15:22-28

22And, behold, a woman of Canaan came out of the same coasts, and cried unto him, saying, Have mercy on me, O Lord, thou son of David; my daughter is grievously vexed with a devil.

23But he answered her not a word. And his disciples came and besought him, saying, Send her away; for she crieth after us.

24But he answered and said, I am not sent but unto the lost sheep of the house of Israel.

25Then came she and worshipped him, saying, Lord, help me.

26But he answered and said, It is not meet to take the children's bread, and to cast it to dogs.

27And she said, Truth, Lord: yet the dogs eat of the crumbs which fall from their masters' table.

28Then Jesus answered and said unto her, O woman, great is thy faith: be it unto thee even as thou wilt. And her daughter was made whole from that very hour.

Matthew 17:19-20

19Then came the disciples to Jesus apart, and said, Why could not we cast him out?

20And Jesus said unto them, Because of your unbelief: for verily I say unto you, If ye have faith as a grain of mustard seed, ye shall say unto this mountain, Remove hence to yonder place; and it shall remove; and nothing shall be impossible unto you.

Matthew 21:19-22

19And when he saw a fig tree in the way, he came to it, and found nothing thereon, but leaves only, and said unto it, Let no fruit grow on thee henceforward for ever. And presently the fig tree withered away.

20And when the disciples saw it, they marvelled, saying, How soon is the fig tree withered away!

21Jesus answered and said unto them, Verily I say unto you, If ye have faith, and doubt not, ye shall not only do this which is done to the fig tree, but also if ye shall say unto this mountain, Be thou removed, and be thou cast into the sea; it shall be done.

[22]And all things, whatsoever ye shall ask in prayer, believing, ye shall receive.

Mark 4:40

[40]And he said unto them, Why are ye so fearful? how is it that ye have no faith?

Mark 5:25-34

[25]And a certain woman, which had an issue of blood twelve years,

[26]And had suffered many things of many physicians, and had spent all that she had, and was nothing bettered, but rather grew worse,

[27]When she had heard of Jesus, came in the press behind, and touched his garment.

[28]For she said, If I may touch but his clothes, I shall be whole.

[29]And straightway the fountain of her blood was dried up; and she felt in her body that she was healed of that plague.

[30]And Jesus, immediately knowing in himself that virtue had gone out of him, turned him about in the press, and said, Who touched my clothes?

[31]And his disciples said unto him, Thou seest the multitude thronging thee, and sayest thou, Who touched me?

[32]And he looked round about to see her that had done this thing.

[33]But the woman fearing and trembling, knowing what was done in her, came and fell down before him, and told him all the truth.

³⁴And he said unto her, Daughter, thy faith hath made thee whole; go in peace, and be whole of thy plague.

Mark 5:36

³⁶As soon as Jesus heard the word that was spoken, he saith unto the ruler of the synagogue, Be not afraid, only believe.

Mark 7:25-30

²⁵For a certain woman, whose young daughter had an unclean spirit, heard of him, and came and fell at his feet:

²⁶The woman was a Greek, a Syrophenician by nation; and she besought him that he would cast forth the devil out of her daughter.

²⁷But Jesus said unto her, Let the children first be filled: for it is not meet to take the children's bread, and to cast it unto the dogs.

²⁸And she answered and said unto him, Yes, Lord: yet the dogs under the table eat of the children's crumbs.

²⁹And he said unto her, For this saying go thy way; the devil is gone out of thy daughter.

³⁰And when she was come to her house, she found the devil gone out, and her daughter laid upon the bed.

Mark 9:23

²³Jesus said unto him, If thou canst believe, all things are possible to him that believeth.

Mark 10:26-27

²⁶And they were astonished out of measure, saying among themselves, Who then can be saved?

²⁷And Jesus looking upon them saith, With men it is impossible, but not with God: for with God all things are possible.

Mark 10:52

⁵²And Jesus said unto him, Go thy way; thy faith hath made thee whole. And immediately he received his sight, and followed Jesus in the way.

Mark 11:22-23

²²And Jesus answering saith unto them, Have faith in God.

²³For verily I say unto you, That whosoever shall say unto this mountain, Be thou removed, and be thou cast into the sea; and shall not doubt in his heart, but shall believe that those things which he saith shall come to pass; he shall have whatsoever he saith.

Mark 12:44

⁴⁴For all they did cast in of their abundance; but she of her want did cast in all that she had, even all her living.

Luke 5:20

²⁰And when he saw their faith, he said unto him, Man, thy sins are forgiven thee.

Luke 7:9

⁹ When Jesus heard these things, he marvelled at him, and turned him about, and said unto the people that followed him, I say unto you, I have not found so great faith, no, not in Israel.

Luke 7:50

⁵⁰And he said to the woman, Thy faith hath saved thee; go in peace.

So You Call Yourself A Christian?

Luke 8:25

25And he said unto them, Where is your faith? And they being afraid wondered, saying one to another, What manner of man is this! for he commandeth even the winds and water, and they obey him.

Luke 8:48

48And he said unto her, Daughter, be of good comfort: thy faith hath made thee whole; go in peace.

Luke 9:41

41And Jesus answering said, O faithless and perverse generation, how long shall I be with you, and suffer you? Bring thy son hither.

Luke 17:19

19And he said unto him, Arise, go thy way: thy faith hath made thee whole.

Luke 18:42

42And Jesus said unto him, Receive thy sight: thy faith hath saved thee.

Matthew 13:57-58

57And they were offended in him. But Jesus said unto them, A prophet is not without honour, save in his own country, and in his own house.

58And he did not many mighty works there because of their unbelief.

Mark 6:4-6

⁴ But Jesus, said unto them, A prophet is not without honour, but in his own country, and among his own kin, and in his own house.

⁵ And he could there do no mighty work, save that he laid his hands upon a few sick folk, and healed them.

⁶ And he marvelled because of their unbelief. And he went round about the villages, teaching.

Luke 4:24

²⁴And he said, Verily I say unto you, No prophet is accepted in his own country.

John 4:44

⁴⁴For Jesus himself testified, that a prophet hath no honour in his own country.

"Thy Faith," is a tremendous pair of words that have never received the recognition and discussion they needed to propel the true believer forward in their faith, their growth to understanding themselves, and in the work and Love of God the Source. In many of the personal instances where a person or a loved one was healed, Jesus said that they were healed because of "Thy Faith". Many times he asked the disciples where is "Your Faith?" or he told them that if they only had a little "Faith...." What does this mean? This means that each individual—you and me—is the starting point of God's actions in our lives. We are the catalyst to the miracles or lack thereof. We are the catalyst to healing or lack thereof. We are the catalyst to forgiveness or lack thereof. These are the words of Christ, "Personal Responsibility", so when does or will the truth begin to shine in your life? Because at present, it doesn't; and that until the current teachings to the masses are thoroughly reconsidered. A litmus test to the truth is this: when, under your current understanding are you going to have dominion over your life—never mind the earth? Let's just talk about your life for now. Under your current understanding, when is it going to be realized? If you cling to your current understanding, it will never be realized. "Thy Faith," clearly indicates that "Personal Responsibility" is the prerequisite to God's Love and power working in your life. Read from the proper perspective and you will see, there are clear indicators throughout the scriptures, especially in the "Teachings of Jesus."

✓ **Inside Out**

In this section we are looking for where spiritual growth occurs, and whether it has anything to do with what we do in our outside, physical experience.

Matthew 4:24

24And his fame went throughout all Syria: and they brought unto him all sick people that were taken with divers diseases and torments, and those which were possessed with devils, and those which were lunatick, and those that had the palsy; and he healed them.

Matthew 6:22-24

22The light of the body is the eye: if therefore thine eye be single, thy whole body shall be full of light.

23But if thine eye be evil, thy whole body shall be full of darkness. If therefore the light that is in thee be darkness, how great is that darkness!

24No man can serve two masters: for either he will hate the one, and love the other; or else he will hold to the one, and despise the other. Ye cannot serve God and mammon.

Matthew 12:33-37

33Either make the tree good, and his fruit good; or else make the tree corrupt, and his fruit corrupt: for the tree is known by his fruit.

34O generation of vipers, how can ye, being evil, speak good things? for out of the abundance of the heart the mouth speaketh.

So You Call Yourself A Christian?

35A good man out of the good treasure of the heart bringeth forth good things: and an evil man out of the evil treasure bringeth forth evil things.

36But I say unto you, That every idle word that men shall speak, they shall give account thereof in the day of judgment.

37For by thy words thou shalt be justified, and by thy words thou shalt be condemned.

Matthew 15:8-9

8 This people draweth nigh unto me with their mouth, and honoureth me with their lips; but their heart is far from me.

9 But in vain they do worship me, teaching for doctrines the commandments of men.

Matthew 15:11

11Not that which goeth into the mouth defileth a man; but that which cometh out of the mouth, this defileth a man.

Matthew 15:17-20

17Do not ye yet understand, that whatsoever entereth in at the mouth goeth into the belly, and is cast out into the draught?

18But those things which proceed out of the mouth come forth from the heart; and they defile the man.

19For out of the heart proceed evil thoughts, murders, adulteries, fornications, thefts, false witness, blasphemies:

20These are the things which defile a man: but to eat with unwashen hands defileth not a man.

Matthew 16:24-26

24Then said Jesus unto his disciples, If any man will come after me, let him deny himself, and take up his cross, and follow me.

25For whosoever will save his life shall lose it: and whosoever will lose his life for my sake shall find it.

26For what is a man profited, if he shall gain the whole world, and lose his own soul? or what shall a man give in exchange for his soul?

Matthew 18:7

7 Woe unto the world because of offences! for it must needs be that offences come; but woe to that man by whom the offence cometh!

Matthew 19:29

29And every one that hath forsaken houses, or brethren, or sisters, or father, or mother, or wife, or children, or lands, for my name's sake, shall receive an hundredfold, and shall inherit everlasting life.

Matthew 22:37-40

37Jesus said unto him, Thou shalt love the Lord thy God with all thy heart, and with all thy soul, and with all thy mind.

38This is the first and great commandment.

39And the second is like unto it, Thou shalt love thy neighbour as thyself.

40On these two commandments hang all the law and the prophets.

So You Call Yourself A Christian?

Matthew 23:25-32

²⁵Woe unto you, scribes and Pharisees, hypocrites! for ye make clean the outside of the cup and of the platter, but within they are full of extortion and excess.

²⁶Thou blind Pharisee, cleanse first that which is within the cup and platter, that the outside of them may be clean also.

²⁷Woe unto you, scribes and Pharisees, hypocrites! for ye are like unto whited sepulchres, which indeed appear beautiful outward, but are within full of dead men's bones, and of all uncleanness.

²⁸Even so ye also outwardly appear righteous unto men, but within ye are full of hypocrisy and iniquity.

²⁹Woe unto you, scribes and Pharisees, hypocrites! because ye build the tombs of the prophets, and garnish the sepulchres of the righteous,

³⁰And say, If we had been in the days of our fathers, we would not have been partakers with them in the blood of the prophets.

³¹Wherefore ye be witnesses unto yourselves, that ye are the children of them which killed the prophets.

³²Fill ye up then the measure of your fathers.

Matthew 24:26

²⁶Wherefore if they shall say unto you, Behold, he is in the desert; go not forth: behold, he is in the secret chambers; believe it not.

Mark 3:23-27

²³And he called them unto him, and said unto them in parables, How can Satan cast out Satan?

24And if a kingdom be divided against itself, that kingdom cannot stand.

25And if a house be divided against itself, that house cannot stand.

26And if Satan rise up against himself, and be divided, he cannot stand, but hath an end.

27No man can enter into a strong man's house, and spoil his goods, except he will first bind the strong man; and then he will spoil his house.

Mark 4:22-24

22For there is nothing hid, which shall not be manifested; neither was any thing kept secret, but that it should come abroad.

23If any man have ears to hear, let him hear.

24And he said unto them, Take heed what ye hear: with what measure ye mete, it shall be measured to you: and unto you that hear shall more be given.

Mark 6:51-52

51And he went up unto them into the ship; and the wind ceased: and they were sore amazed in themselves beyond measure, and wondered.

52For they considered not the miracle of the loaves: for their heart was hardened.

Mark 7:18-23

18And he saith unto them, Are ye so without understanding also? Do ye not perceive, that whatsoever thing from without entereth into the man, it cannot defile him;

¹⁹Because it entereth not into his heart, but into the belly, and goeth out into the draught, purging all meats?

²⁰And he said, That which cometh out of the man, that defileth the man.

²¹For from within, out of the heart of men, proceed evil thoughts, adulteries, fornications, murders,

²²Thefts, covetousness, wickedness, deceit, lasciviousness, an evil eye, blasphemy, pride, foolishness:

²³All these evil things come from within, and defile the man.

Mark 8:34-37

³⁴And when he had called the people unto him with his disciples also, he said unto them, Whosoever will come after me, let him deny himself, and take up his cross, and follow me.

³⁵For whosoever will save his life shall lose it; but whosoever shall lose his life for my sake and the gospel's, the same shall save it.

³⁶For what shall it profit a man, if he shall gain the whole world, and lose his own soul?

³⁷Or what shall a man give in exchange for his soul?

Mark 12:31-34

³⁰And thou shalt love the Lord thy God with all thy heart, and with all thy soul, and with all thy mind, and with all thy strength: this is the first commandment.

³¹And the second is like, namely this, Thou shalt love thy neighbour as thyself. There is none other commandment greater than these.

³²And the scribe said unto him, Well, Master, thou hast said the truth: for there is one God; and there is none other but he:

33And to love him with all the heart, and with all the understanding, and with all the soul, and with all the strength, and to love his neighbour as himself, is more than all whole burnt offerings and sacrifices.

34And when Jesus saw that he answered discreetly, he said unto him, Thou art not far from the kingdom of God. And no man after that durst ask him any question.

Luke 6:41-45

41And why beholdest thou the mote that is in thy brother's eye, but perceivest not the beam that is in thine own eye?

42Either how canst thou say to thy brother, Brother, let me pull out the mote that is in thine eye, when thou thyself beholdest not the beam that is in thine own eye? Thou hypocrite, cast out first the beam out of thine own eye, and then shalt thou see clearly to pull out the mote that is in thy brother's eye.

43For a good tree bringeth not forth corrupt fruit; neither doth a corrupt tree bring forth good fruit.

44For every tree is known by his own fruit. For of thorns men do not gather figs, nor of a bramble bush gather they grapes.

45A good man out of the good treasure of his heart bringeth forth that which is good; and an evil man out of the evil treasure of his heart bringeth forth that which is evil: for of the abundance of the heart his mouth speaketh.

Luke 8:11

11Now the parable is this: The seed is the word of God.

Luke 11:39-54

39And the Lord said unto him, Now do ye Pharisees make clean the outside of the cup and the platter; but your inward part is full of ravening and wickedness.

40Ye fools, did not he that made that which is without make that which is within also?

41But rather give alms of such things as ye have; and, behold, all things are clean unto you.

42But woe unto you, Pharisees! for ye tithe mint and rue and all manner of herbs, and pass over judgment and the love of God: these ought ye to have done, and not to leave the other undone.

43Woe unto you, Pharisees! for ye love the uppermost seats in the synagogues, and greetings in the markets.

44Woe unto you, scribes and Pharisees, hypocrites! for ye are as graves which appear not, and the men that walk over them are not aware of them.

45Then answered one of the lawyers, and said unto him, Master, thus saying thou reproachest us also.

46And he said, Woe unto you also, ye lawyers! for ye lade men with burdens grievous to be borne, and ye yourselves touch not the burdens with one of your fingers.

47Woe unto you! for ye build the sepulchres of the prophets, and your fathers killed them.

48Truly ye bear witness that ye allow the deeds of your fathers: for they indeed killed them, and ye build their sepulchres.

49Therefore also said the wisdom of God, I will send them prophets and apostles, and some of them they shall slay and persecute:

50That the blood of all the prophets, which was shed from the foundation of the world, may be required of this generation;

51From the blood of Abel unto the blood of Zacharias which perished between the altar and the temple: verily I say unto you, It shall be required of this generation.

[52]Woe unto you, lawyers! for ye have taken away the key of knowledge: ye entered not in yourselves, and them that were entering in ye hindered.

[53]And as he said these things unto them, the scribes and the Pharisees began to urge him vehemently, and to provoke him to speak of many things:

[54]Laying wait for him, and seeking to catch something out of his mouth, that they might accuse him.

Luke 14:26-27

[26]If any man come to me, and hate not his father, and mother, and wife, and children, and brethren, and sisters, yea, and his own life also, he cannot be my disciple.

[27]And whosoever doth not bear his cross, and come after me, cannot be my disciple.

Luke 16:15

[15]And he said unto them, Ye are they which justify yourselves before men; but God knoweth your hearts: for that which is highly esteemed among men is abomination in the sight of God.

Luke 18:16-17

[16]But Jesus called them unto him, and said, Suffer little children to come unto me, and forbid them not: for of such is the kingdom of God.

[17]Verily I say unto you, Whosoever shall not receive the kingdom of God as a little child shall in no wise enter therein.

So You Call Yourself A Christian?

Luke 18:29-30

²⁹And he said unto them, Verily I say unto you, There is no man that hath left house, or parents, or brethren, or wife, or children, for the kingdom of God's sake,

³⁰Who shall not receive manifold more in this present time, and in the world to come life everlasting.

John 3:3-8

³ Jesus answered and said unto him, Verily, verily, I say unto thee, Except a man be born again, he cannot see the kingdom of God.

⁴ Nicodemus saith unto him, How can a man be born when he is old? can he enter the second time into his mother's womb, and be born?

⁵ Jesus answered, Verily, verily, I say unto thee, Except a man be born of water and of the Spirit, he cannot enter into the kingdom of God.

⁶ That which is born of the flesh is flesh; and that which is born of the Spirit is spirit.

⁷ Marvel not that I said unto thee, Ye must be born again.

⁸ The wind bloweth where it listeth, and thou hearest the sound thereof, but canst not tell whence it cometh, and whither it goeth: so is every one that is born of the Spirit.

John 3:19-21

¹⁹And this is the condemnation, that light is come into the world, and men loved darkness rather than light, because their deeds were evil.

²⁰For every one that doeth evil hateth the light, neither cometh to the light, lest his deeds should be reproved.

21But he that doeth truth cometh to the light, that his deeds may be made manifest, that they are wrought in God.

John 4:23-24

3 But the hour cometh, and now is, when the true worshippers shall worship the Father in spirit and in truth: for the Father seeketh such to worship him.

24God is a Spirit: and they that worship him must worship him in spirit and in truth.

John 5:38

38And ye have not his word abiding in you: for whom he hath sent, him ye believe not.

John 6:48-58

48I am that bread of life.

49Your fathers did eat manna in the wilderness, and are dead.

50This is the bread which cometh down from heaven, that a man may eat thereof, and not die.

51I am the living bread which came down from heaven: if any man eat of this bread, he shall live for ever: and the bread that I will give is my flesh, which I will give for the life of the world.

52The Jews therefore strove among themselves, saying, How can this man give us his flesh to eat?

53Then Jesus said unto them, Verily, verily, I say unto you, Except ye eat the flesh of the Son of man, and drink his blood, ye have no life in you.

54Whoso eateth my flesh, and drinketh my blood, hath eternal life; and I will raise him up at the last day.

⁵⁵For my flesh is meat indeed, and my blood is drink indeed.

⁵⁶He that eateth my flesh, and drinketh my blood, dwelleth in me, and I in him.

⁵⁷As the living Father hath sent me, and I live by the Father: so he that eateth me, even he shall live by me.

⁵⁸This is that bread which came down from heaven: not as your fathers did eat manna, and are dead: he that eateth of this bread shall live for ever.

John 6:63

⁶³It is the spirit that quickeneth; the flesh profiteth nothing: the words that I speak unto you, they are spirit, and they are life.

John 7:38

³⁸He that believeth on me, as the scripture hath said, out of his belly shall flow rivers of living water.

John 13:34-35

³⁴A new commandment I give unto you, That ye love one another; as I have loved you, that ye also love one another.

³⁵By this shall all men know that ye are my disciples, if ye have love one to another.

John 15:3

³ Now ye are clean through the word which I have spoken unto you.

John 15:4-8

⁴ Abide in me, and I in you. As the branch cannot bear fruit of itself, except it abide in the vine; no more can ye, except ye abide in me.

⁵ I am the vine, ye are the branches: He that abideth in me, and I in him, the same bringeth forth much fruit: for without me ye can do nothing.

⁶ If a man abide not in me, he is cast forth as a branch, and is withered; and men gather them, and cast them into the fire, and they are burned.

⁷ If ye abide in me, and my words abide in you, ye shall ask what ye will, and it shall be done unto you.

⁸ Herein is my Father glorified, that ye bear much fruit; so shall ye be my disciples.

Here the "Teachings of Jesus", make very plain that the work involved, or the process of growth is an inside job. Each of these beautiful scriptures directs you to a work done on the inside, a changing done on the inside, a cleansing done on the inside. Few have realized the truth and power of this, because few have done the necessary work. Few have truly bore their cross. Few have engaged their habits, their current ways of thinking, speaking, and acting, to change and align themselves with the thinking, words, and actions of God. Why is this important? It is important because for hundreds of years, thousands if not millions of individuals have rested on the fact that they accepted someone as their personal savior, and being baptized—which is only an outward depiction of something that should be done on the inside—is all that they had to do. Yet, it should be the beginning. You cannot say, "I accept someone," in truth, "Their Teachings"," and go home to the same habits, to the same way of doing things, to the same way of speaking. You have not bore your cross, you have done no work, and you have put forth no effort. Each of us is charged with the job of reconnecting with God the Source of all. Maps have been placed in the world to follow. They will take us to the only true destination toward which we should be journeying. "Jesus' Teachings" are just that type of map, however they specifically imply a grand measure of "Personal Responsibility" in the matter, and if you are currently, actively on the path, you will come to the truth of this for yourself at some point. But, if you are passively riding the Flow of Life, thinking that things are being done to you by a God that supposedly Loves you, you will never realize the truth because you have yet to take any responsibility in the matter as a Child of God, as a child of a King most absolutely would.

✓ **Jesus Implying Separation from God – God is Master**

In this section we are observing whether Jesus states we are truly accepting him, or God who sent him. Who is master, even Christ's master?

Matthew 19:17

17And he said unto him, Why callest thou me good? there is none good but one, that is, God: but if thou wilt enter into life, keep the commandments.

Matthew 20:23

23And he saith unto them, Ye shall drink indeed of my cup, and be baptized with the baptism that I am baptized with: but to sit on my right hand, and on my left, is not mine to give, but it shall be given to them for whom it is prepared of my Father.

Matthew 23:8-12

8 But be not ye called Rabbi: for one is your Master, even Christ; and all ye are brethren.

9 And call no man your father upon the earth: for one is your Father, which is in heaven.

10Neither be ye called masters: for one is your Master, even Christ.

11But he that is greatest among you shall be your servant.

12And whosoever shall exalt himself shall be abased; and he that shall humble himself shall be exalted.

So You Call Yourself A Christian?

Mark 9:37

[37]Whosoever shall receive one of such children in my name, receiveth me: and whosoever shall receive me, receiveth not me, but him that sent me.

Mark 10:37-45

[37]They said unto him, Grant unto us that we may sit, one on thy right hand, and the other on thy left hand, in thy glory.

[38]But Jesus said unto them, Ye know not what ye ask: can ye drink of the cup that I drink of? and be baptized with the baptism that I am baptized with?

[39]And they said unto him, We can. And Jesus said unto them, Ye shall indeed drink of the cup that I drink of; and with the baptism that I am baptized withal shall ye be baptized:

[40]But to sit on my right hand and on my left hand is not mine to give; but it shall be given to them for whom it is prepared.

[41]And when the ten heard it, they began to be much displeased with James and John.

[42]But Jesus called them to him, and saith unto them, Ye know that they which are accounted to rule over the Gentiles exercise lordship over them; and their great ones exercise authority upon them.

[43]But so shall it not be among you: but whosoever will be great among you, shall be your minister:

[44]And whosoever of you will be the chiefest, shall be servant of all.

[45]For even the Son of man came not to be ministered unto, but to minister, and to give his life a ransom for many.

John 12:44-48

44Jesus cried and said, He that believeth on me, believeth not on me, but on him that sent me.

45And he that seeth me seeth him that sent me.

46I am come a light into the world, that whosoever believeth on me should not abide in darkness.

47And if any man hear my words, and believe not, I judge him not: for I came not to judge the world, but to save the world.

48He that rejecteth me, and receiveth not my words, hath one that judgeth him: the word that I have spoken, the same shall judge him in the last day.

John 14:7, 10-12

7 If ye had known me, ye should have known my Father also: and from henceforth ye know him, and have seen him.

10Believest thou not that I am in the Father, and the Father in me? the words that I speak unto you I speak not of myself: but the Father that dwelleth in me, he doeth the works.

11Believe me that I am in the Father, and the Father in me: or else believe me for the very works' sake.

12Verily, verily, I say unto you, He that believeth on me, the works that I do shall he do also; and greater works than these shall he do; because I go unto my Father.

The separation that Jesus implies in these scriptures carries a two fold meaning. First, Jesus makes plain that only God is good. He also makes it understood that God is Master, that God is his master as well as ours, and that God the Father is the goal, or what we are connecting with. Jesus directly speaks of the separation between himself and God when the disciples

asked if they could sit at his right and his left hand, and he says that it is not for him to give, it is only for him whom it is prepared.

The greater message of Jesus' implying separation between him and God is that God has been all along, has always been present, and always will be. The mission of "Jesus' Teachings", Jesus' coming, was to be a guide to those who have become lost through misguidance and misunderstanding. He also stated in other scriptures to the heads of the church that they had silenced the true meanings of the scriptures, and had not entered the "Strait Gate." As a result they had kept everyone else from passing through the gate. This travesty was a tactic that continues to be employed, because if a person realizes the true meanings of the scriptures, it threatens the organization of religion, the same as it did in Jesus' time. Come to know the God that has always been. The God that was before any scriptures ever were, and the God that will reside in all things when there is nothing. This is the reason Jesus implied separation, because he was merely doing the work that was given to him by all that is and all that was, as we all must do.

✓ **Law at Work – Whatever You Ask, Whether Good or Evil**

In this section, we begin to observe that Law is governing our being. Those things, which we are being and doing unto others, as well as to our inner most thoughts and beliefs, are of our own asking. We are receiving what we are asking.

Matthew 7:7-12

⁷ Ask, and it shall be given you; seek, and ye shall find; knock, and it shall be opened unto you:

⁸ For every one that asketh receiveth; and he that seeketh findeth; and to him that knocketh it shall be opened.

⁹ Or what man is there of you, whom if his son ask bread, will he give him a stone?

¹⁰Or if he ask a fish, will he give him a serpent?

¹¹If ye then, being evil, know how to give good gifts unto your children, how much more shall your Father which is in heaven give good things to them that ask him?

¹²Therefore all things whatsoever ye would that men should do to you, do ye even so to them: for this is the law and the prophets.

Mark 11:24-26

²⁴Therefore I say unto you, What things soever ye desire, when ye pray, believe that ye receive them, and ye shall have them.

²⁵And when ye stand praying, forgive, if ye have ought against any: that your Father also which is in heaven may forgive you your trespasses.

26But if ye do not forgive, neither will your Father which is in heaven forgive your trespasses.

Luke 6:36-38

36Be ye therefore merciful, as your Father also is merciful.

37Judge not, and ye shall not be judged: condemn not, and ye shall not be condemned: forgive, and ye shall be forgiven:

38Give, and it shall be given unto you; good measure, pressed down, and shaken together, and running over, shall men give into your bosom. For with the same measure that ye mete withal it shall be measured to you again.

Yes, my beloved, that which we all have thought was God for so long is not actually God, but God's Law that is put in place to govern our being. Jesus makes mention of this all through many points of his teachings and solidifies it when he states that "God sends rain to the just and the unjust."
"He sends sun to the good and evil alike."

So what does this mean? Again, we are governed by "Law", and not by an entity that is taking notes on our every action and at the same time is sending us pain and suffering. No, No, NO! We are choosing whether to abide by, and work with God's Law or we are not. We are choosing to walk in the "Light", or we are not. We are choosing to enter the "Strait Gate", and "Walk the Narrow Path", or we are not. In our choosing or not choosing, "We Are Choosing", and the results that we achieve are either lined and coated on a foundation of LOVE, or they are lined and coated on a foundation of pain and suffering.

"Ask," "Ask," "Ask…!" This is the question and the key to all that you want. So why are you not getting what you want? You are. Your asking is tied to your focus and not just the words that come out of the mouth every time you change your mind. We say we want wealth and increase but we are focused on the fact that we do not have enough to pay our bills or to help our neighbor. Your dominant focus is what you are asking for. We say we want great relationships and/or a great marriage. However, we do not want to be cheated on, controlled, or lied to. If the dominant focus is on cheating, controlling, or lying, that is what you are asking for, and that is what you are getting and have always received. Whatever lies within your innermost being, as deep, and deeper than the subconscious mind, is what we are asking for and receiving— nothing more and nothing less—all the time. This is law; not every once and a while allowances from God the Source.

The final point to remember and to know in this introduction to the "Law", of which Jesus speaks, is the fact that each of us has a "Personal Choice" in our lives and no matter what we have been asking and receiving to this point, we can change it. We can change it by consciously choosing and directing our thoughts, and by finely evaluating the thoughts that randomly pass through our minds as to whether we accept them as being true for us at this moment in our growth and understanding about ourselves. Do you believe that the economy is bad "For You"? If you do, it will be so. Do you believe it is hard to make money? If you do, it will be so. Do you believe that it is difficult to find a mate, partner, husband or wife? If you do, it will be so. To know the truth of this, you simply have to look around you and see if what you believe to be true is true for everyone. If it is not true for everyone, it is only a belief that you hold, and it can be changed. In its changing, it will yield new and different life results, because you are now working with, aligning with, and directing "Universal Law". As a "Child of God the Source", you can do that.

✓ **Do**

In this section we are observing whether anything less that "Doing" the word of God is acceptable.

Matthew 7:24

²⁴Therefore whosoever heareth these sayings of mine, and doeth them, I will liken him unto a wise man, which built his house upon a rock:

Matthew 24:46-51

⁴⁶Blessed is that servant, whom his lord when he cometh shall find so doing.

⁴⁷Verily I say unto you, That he shall make him ruler over all his goods.

⁴⁸But and if that evil servant shall say in his heart, My lord delayeth his coming;

⁴⁹And shall begin to smite his fellowservants, and to eat and drink with the drunken;

⁵⁰The lord of that servant shall come in a day when he looketh not for him, and in an hour that he is not aware of,

⁵¹And shall cut him asunder, and appoint him his portion with the hypocrites: there shall be weeping and gnashing of teeth.

Mark 7:1-13

¹ Then came together unto him the Pharisees, and certain of the scribes, which came from Jerusalem.

² And when they saw some of his disciples eat bread with defiled, that is to say, with unwashen, hands, they found fault.

³ For the Pharisees, and all the Jews, except they wash their hands oft, eat not, holding the tradition of the elders.

⁴ And when they come from the market, except they wash, they eat not. And many other things there be, which they have received to hold, as the washing of cups, and pots, brasen vessels, and of tables.

⁵ Then the Pharisees and scribes asked him, Why walk not thy disciples according to the tradition of the elders, but eat bread with unwashen hands?

⁶ He answered and said unto them, Well hath Esaias prophesied of you hypocrites, as it is written, This people honoureth me with their lips, but their heart is far from me.

⁷ Howbeit in vain do they worship me, teaching for doctrines the commandments of men.

⁸ For laying aside the commandment of God, ye hold the tradition of men, as the washing of pots and cups: and many other such like things ye do.

⁹ And he said unto them, Full well ye reject the commandment of God, that ye may keep your own tradition.

¹⁰For Moses said, Honour thy father and thy mother; and, Whoso curseth father or mother, let him die the death:

¹¹But ye say, If a man shall say to his father or mother, It is Corban, that is to say, a gift, by whatsoever thou mightest be profited by me; he shall be free.

¹²And ye suffer him no more to do ought for his father or his mother;

¹³Making the word of God of none effect through your tradition, which ye have delivered: and many such like things do ye.

So You Call Yourself A Christian?

Mark 9:38-40

[38]And John answered him, saying, Master, we saw one casting out devils in thy name, and he followeth not us: and we forbad him, because he followeth not us.

[39]But Jesus said, Forbid him not: for there is no man which shall do a miracle in my name, that can lightly speak evil of me.

[40]For he that is not against us is on our part.

Mark 10:27-31

[27]And Jesus looking upon them saith, With men it is impossible, but not with God: for with God all things are possible.

[28]Then Peter began to say unto him, Lo, we have left all, and have followed thee.

[29]And Jesus answered and said, Verily I say unto you, There is no man that hath left house, or brethren, or sisters, or father, or mother, or wife, or children, or lands, for my sake, and the gospel's,

[30]But he shall receive an hundredfold now in this time, houses, and brethren, and sisters, and mothers, and children, and lands, with persecutions; and in the world to come eternal life.

[31]But many that are first shall be last; and the last first.

Luke 6:35

[35]But love ye your enemies, and do good, and lend, hoping for nothing again; and your reward shall be great, and ye shall be the children of the Highest: for he is kind unto the unthankful and to the evil.

Luke 6:46-49

[46]And why call ye me, Lord, Lord, and do not the things which I say?

⁴⁷Whosoever cometh to me, and heareth my sayings, and doeth them, I will shew you to whom he is like:

⁴⁸He is like a man which built an house, and digged deep, and laid the foundation on a rock: and when the flood arose, the stream beat vehemently upon that house, and could not shake it: for it was founded upon a rock.

⁴⁹But he that heareth, and doeth not, is like a man that without a foundation built an house upon the earth; against which the stream did beat vehemently, and immediately it fell; and the ruin of that house was great.

Luke 7:47

⁴⁷Wherefore I say unto thee, Her sins, which are many, are forgiven; for she loved much: but to whom little is forgiven, the same loveth little.

Luke 9:49-50

⁴⁹And John answered and said, Master, we saw one casting out devils in thy name; and we forbad him, because he followeth not with us.

⁵⁰And Jesus said unto him, Forbid him not: for he that is not against us is for us.

Luke 10:25-37

²⁵And, behold, a certain lawyer stood up, and tempted him, saying, Master, what shall I do to inherit eternal life?

²⁶He said unto him, What is written in the law? how readest thou?

²⁷And he answering said, Thou shalt love the Lord thy God with all thy heart, and with all thy soul, and with all thy strength, and with all thy mind; and thy neighbour as thyself.

²⁸And he said unto him, Thou hast answered right: this do, and thou shalt live.

²⁹But he, willing to justify himself, said unto Jesus, And who is my neighbour?

³⁰And Jesus answering said, A certain man went down from Jerusalem to Jericho, and fell among thieves, which stripped him of his raiment, and wounded him, and departed, leaving him half dead.

³¹And by chance there came down a certain priest that way: and when he saw him, he passed by on the other side.

³²And likewise a Levite, when he was at the place, came and looked on him, and passed by on the other side.

³³But a certain Samaritan, as he journeyed, came where he was: and when he saw him, he had compassion on him,

³⁴And went to him, and bound up his wounds, pouring in oil and wine, and set him on his own beast, and brought him to an inn, and took care of him.

³⁵And on the morrow when he departed, he took out two pence, and gave them to the host, and said unto him, Take care of him; and whatsoever thou spendest more, when I come again, I will repay thee.

³⁶Which now of these three, thinkest thou, was neighbour unto him that fell among the thieves?

³⁷And he said, He that shewed mercy on him. Then said Jesus unto him, Go, and do thou likewise.

Luke 11:28

²⁸But he said, Yea rather, blessed are they that hear the word of God, and keep it.

Luke 12:36-48

[36]And ye yourselves like unto men that wait for their lord, when he will return from the wedding; that when he cometh and knocketh, they may open unto him immediately.

[37]Blessed are those servants, whom the lord when he cometh shall find watching: verily I say unto you, that he shall gird himself, and make them to sit down to meat, and will come forth and serve them.

[38]And if he shall come in the second watch, or come in the third watch, and find them so, blessed are those servants.

[39]And this know, that if the goodman of the house had known what hour the thief would come, he would have watched, and not have suffered his house to be broken through.

[40]Be ye therefore ready also: for the Son of man cometh at an hour when ye think not.

[41]Then Peter said unto him, Lord, speakest thou this parable unto us, or even to all?

[42]And the Lord said, Who then is that faithful and wise steward, whom his lord shall make ruler over his household, to give them their portion of meat in due season?

[43]Blessed is that servant, whom his lord when he cometh shall find so doing.

[44]Of a truth I say unto you, that he will make him ruler over all that he hath.

[45]But and if that servant say in his heart, My lord delayeth his coming; and shall begin to beat the menservants and maidens, and to eat and drink, and to be drunken;

[46]The lord of that servant will come in a day when he looketh not for him, and at an hour when he is not aware, and will cut him in sunder, and will appoint him his portion with the unbelievers.

⁴⁷And that servant, which knew his lord's will, and prepared not himself, neither did according to his will, shall be beaten with many stripes.

⁴⁸But he that knew not, and did commit things worthy of stripes, shall be beaten with few stripes. For unto whomsoever much is given, of him shall be much required: and to whom men have committed much, of him they will ask the more.

John 8:31-32

³¹Then said Jesus to those Jews which believed on him, If ye continue in my word, then are ye my disciples indeed;

³²And ye shall know the truth, and the truth shall make you free.

John 8:51

⁵¹Verily, verily, I say unto you, If a man keep my saying, he shall never see death.

John 14:23-24

²³Jesus answered and said unto him, If a man love me, he will keep my words: and my Father will love him, and we will come unto him, and make our abode with him.

²⁴He that loveth me not keepeth not my sayings: and the word which ye hear is not mine, but the Father's which sent me.

Luke 17:5-10

⁵ And the apostles said unto the Lord, Increase our faith.

⁶ And the Lord said, If ye had faith as a grain of mustard seed, ye might say unto this sycamine tree, Be thou plucked up by the root, and be thou planted in the sea; and it should obey you.

⁷ But which of you, having a servant plowing or feeding cattle, will say unto him by and by, when he is come from the field, Go and sit down to meat?

⁸ And will not rather say unto him, Make ready wherewith I may sup, and gird thyself, and serve me, till I have eaten and drunken; and afterward thou shalt eat and drink?

⁹ Doth he thank that servant because he did the things that were commanded him? I trow not.

¹⁰So likewise ye, when ye shall have done all those things which are commanded you, say, We are unprofitable servants: we have done that which was our duty to do.

The doing of the "Teachings of Jesus", are the downfall of all who follow. It is the downfall of all who claim and carry the title of "Christian", as if that alone saves them. Sadly enough this is the belief, and the belief, that the pain and suffering of the world, of this physical experience, is part of the ride, is just as disturbing. In this new clarity, this new understanding that you now have, you can see that few are attempting to "Do" the teachings. Many, many are listening, but on so many it has been lost that there should be a "Do" involved. There is no salvation without the "Do." Without the "Do", we are like everyone else who does not have faith, and who is not connected to God the Source. Our lives and the many events that follow illustrate that fact. All through Jesus' teachings, he iterates that those who truly Love him "Keep his Commandments, Follow his word, Do that which has been given." Understand, tomorrow comes whether we want it to or not, whether we like it or not, but the grand "Teachings of Jesus", will always stand as true, and the power that resides in the words will only be realized when we Act, Do, and Follow their direction. Jesus' purpose was to bring the message, to bring the Gospel, to bring the "Good News". It was not to die. Yes, the prophets before him knew that he would be killed, and so did he, but that was not his mission. Jesus died because his teachings threatened their current way of doing things, but they were too late, because he left each of us with direct, precise guidelines to follow and realize the truth of God the Source, and to realize the truth of ourselves.

Summary:

This chapter clearly indicates the type of person who is an open channel for God the Source. It also clearly outlines where the responsibility lies when it comes to reconnecting with God. All work, when it comes to God, is an inside job. Just as your personal beauty, strength, and power must be realized on the inside before it can ever be realized on the outside, so must everything that is less than Love in your current ways of thinking, speaking, and acting be removed before God can be realized and experienced in you. Jesus attempted to imply the separation between he and God, saying that only God was good and that God was Master, to indicate that God was the goal and not himself. In the end it comes down to the doing. This is the mandate of Christ—to follow the "Teachings", to allow them to grow in your inner most being, so that the Kingdom might be realized and spring forth from you into the world. The mandate is not to wait on Jesus, but to apply and realize the truth within you, with the help of the Holy Spirit, that God might be your guide because you have trekked your way back to LOVE itself. The mandate is strong, it is ironclad, and it will never change. If you are not disciplined and focused in your efforts to work your way back to perfection, you are doomed to flounder through this life, lost, confused, and in pain.

Chapter II

Kingdom of Heaven! Where?

In the following scriptures, we are observing and recognizing just where the "Kingdom of God", the "Kingdom of Heaven", is to be found. Is it out there somewhere, or is it in here somewhere?

In this section we recognize that when the word of God is sewn and takes root in our hearts (inner most being), the kingdom grows from inside each of us and bears fruit in our lives.

> ✓ **Parable of the Sower – Jesus speaking to the multitude and the disciples**

Matthew 13:18-23

¹⁸Hear ye therefore the parable of the sower.

¹⁹When any one heareth the word of the kingdom, and understandeth it not, then cometh the wicked one, and catcheth away that which was sown in his heart. This is he which received seed by the way side.

²⁰But he that received the seed into stony places, the same is he that heareth the word, and anon with joy receiveth it;

²¹Yet hath he not root in himself, but dureth for a while: for when tribulation or persecution ariseth because of the word, by and by he is offended.

22He also that received seed among the thorns is he that heareth the word; and the care of this world, and the deceitfulness of riches, choke the word, and he becometh unfruitful.

23But he that received seed into the good ground is he that heareth the word, and understandeth it; which also beareth fruit, and bringeth forth, some an hundredfold, some sixty, some thirty.

Mark 4:14-19

14The sower soweth the word.

15And these are they by the way side, where the word is sown; but when they have heard, Satan cometh immediately, and taketh away the word that was sown in their hearts.

16And these are they likewise which are sown on stony ground; who, when they have heard the word, immediately receive it with gladness;

17And have no root in themselves, and so endure but for a time: afterward, when affliction or persecution ariseth for the word's sake, immediately they are offended.

18And these are they which are sown among thorns; such as hear the word,

19And the cares of this world, and the deceitfulness of riches, and the lusts of other things entering in, choke the word, and it becometh unfruitful. **20**And these are they which are sown on good ground; such as hear the word, and receive it, and bring forth fruit, some thirtyfold, some sixty, and some an hundred.

The "Parable of the Sower" is often times looked at as a parable pertaining to the types of people into which the word of God is sewn. However, this parable actually speaks to the type of ground, field, garden that each of us has allowed ourselves to

become. I say *allowed* because there has always been a choice. Behind every thought, behind every word, behind every action there has been a choice for you and for me to make. Now that we are conscious of this, of our responsibility in the matter, we must put the work behind the sowing, in order to fertilize and cultivate the growing of the "Kingdom of God" from our inner most being. This is what is called for at the moment. This is where the change, which you have been asking for, begins in your life.

✓ **Parable of Householder – Jesus speaking to disciples**

In this section, we observe that you get in life exactly what you accept or agree to receive, nothing more and nothing less.

Matthew 20:1-15

¹ For the kingdom of heaven is like unto a man that is an householder, which went out early in the morning to hire labourers into his vineyard.

² And when he had agreed with the labourers for a penny a day, he sent them into his vineyard.

³ And he went out about the third hour, and saw others standing idle in the marketplace,

⁴ And said unto them; Go ye also into the vineyard, and whatsoever is right I will give you. And they went their way.

⁵ Again he went out about the sixth and ninth hour, and did likewise.

⁶ And about the eleventh hour he went out, and found others standing idle, and saith unto them, Why stand ye here all the day idle?

⁷ They say unto him, Because no man hath hired us. He saith unto them, Go ye also into the vineyard; and whatsoever is right, that shall ye receive.

⁸ So when even was come, the lord of the vineyard saith unto his steward, Call the labourers, and give them their hire, beginning from the last unto the first.

⁹ And when they came that were hired about the eleventh hour, they received every man a penny.

¹⁰But when the first came, they supposed that they should have received more; and they likewise received every man a penny.

¹¹And when they had received it, they murmured against the goodman of the house,

¹²Saying, These last have wrought but one hour, and thou hast made them equal unto us, which have borne the burden and heat of the day.

¹³But he answered one of them, and said, Friend, I do thee no wrong: didst not thou agree with me for a penny?

¹⁴Take that thine is, and go thy way: I will give unto this last, even as unto thee.

¹⁵Is it not lawful for me to do what I will with mine own? Is thine eye evil, because I am good?

The "Parable of the Householder", likens the "Kingdom of God" to one who is hiring help for an infinite amount of work. With heaven, "The Kingdom of God", everything that is rewarded or paid is the agreed upon amount and that amount is exactly what you ask for whether consciously or unconsciously. You are getting exactly what you are thinking, feeling, and being. You are getting exactly what you are talking about and believing to be true. Exactly! Entering the "Kingdom of God", the path to the "Kingdom of Heaven", means your thoughts, words, and actions begin to come from the point of LOVE, Unconditional Love, which in turn means the rewards that you receive as fair, agreed upon payment, will be in line with what you truly need and want, and they will be in line with the best that God the Source has to offer.

✓ **Parable of the Ten Virgins – Jesus speaking to the disciples**

In this section we observe the importance of being prepared for the coming or the opening of the Kingdom to us. This preparation is maintaining purity and focus of heart.

Matthew 25:1-13

¹ Then shall the kingdom of heaven be likened unto ten virgins, which took their lamps, and went forth to meet the bridegroom.

² And five of them were wise, and five were foolish.

³ They that were foolish took their lamps, and took no oil with them:

⁴ But the wise took oil in their vessels with their lamps.

⁵ While the bridegroom tarried, they all slumbered and slept.

⁶ And at midnight there was a cry made, Behold, the bridegroom cometh; go ye out to meet him.

⁷ Then all those virgins arose, and trimmed their lamps.

⁸ And the foolish said unto the wise, Give us of your oil; for our lamps are gone out.

⁹ But the wise answered, saying, Not so; lest there be not enough for us and you: but go ye rather to them that sell, and buy for yourselves.

¹⁰And while they went to buy, the bridegroom came; and they that were ready went in with him to the marriage: and the door was shut.

11Afterward came also the other virgins, saying, Lord, Lord, open to us.

12But he answered and said, Verily I say unto you, I know you not.

13Watch therefore, for ye know neither the day nor the hour wherein the Son of man cometh.

The "Kingdom of Heaven" is likened to ten virgins who know exactly what to do and how to become and remain prepared. As you are contaminated from birth of the mind and heart, you must continually trim and fuel your lamp with the scriptures of old until it begins to burn bright and pure, while realizing that the source of your strength, your spiritual power, your spirit, is only different from God the Source in quantity and not quality. In doing so, you walk the narrow path and enter the straight gate to the "Kingdom of Heaven", for it is present always within. The bridegroom is the Kingdom, ready to marry, join, become "One" with all who are prepared and ready.

✓ **Parable of the Man Travelling into a Far Country –
Jesus speaking to disciples**

**In this section, we recognize that the Kingdom multiplies our
talents as we use them, not if we hide them.**

Matthew 25:14-30

14For the kingdom of heaven is as a man travelling into a far
country, who called his own servants, and delivered unto
them his goods.

15And unto one he gave five talents, to another two, and to
another one; to every man according to his several ability;
and straightway took his journey.

16Then he that had received the five talents went and traded
with the same, and made them other five talents.

17And likewise he that had received two, he also gained other
two.

18But he that had received one went and digged in the earth,
and hid his lord's money.

19After a long time the lord of those servants cometh, and
reckoneth with them.

20And so he that had received five talents came and brought
other five talents, saying, Lord, thou deliveredst unto me five
talents: behold, I have gained beside them five talents more.

21His lord said unto him, Well done, thou good and faithful
servant: thou hast been faithful over a few things, I will make
thee ruler over many things: enter thou into the joy of thy
lord.

22He also that had received two talents came and said, Lord,
thou deliveredst unto me two talents: behold, I have gained
two other talents beside them.

23His lord said unto him, Well done, good and faithful servant; thou hast been faithful over a few things, I will make thee ruler over many things: enter thou into the joy of thy lord.

24Then he which had received the one talent came and said, Lord, I knew thee that thou art an hard man, reaping where thou hast not sown, and gathering where thou hast not strawed:

25And I was afraid, and went and hid thy talent in the earth: lo, there thou hast that is thine.

26His lord answered and said unto him, Thou wicked and slothful servant, thou knewest that I reap where I sowed not, and gather where I have not strawed:

27Thou oughtest therefore to have put my money to the exchangers, and then at my coming I should have received mine own with usury.

28Take therefore the talent from him, and give it unto him which hath ten talents.

29For unto every one that hath shall be given, and he shall have abundance: but from him that hath not shall be taken away even that which he hath.

30And cast ye the unprofitable servant into outer darkness: there shall be weeping and gnashing of teeth.

This parable likens the "Kingdom of God" to a man, who is traveling into a far country, who calls his servants, and delivers his goods unto them. Every good leader endows those around him with everything they need to perform their tasks. God the Source has placed within each of us different wants and desires, but He has given each of us the same strength, and the same creative ability, such as prescribed by "Law." The scriptures of the world indicate how to work in unison, in accord with that

"Law", and in doing so, your works and rewards are multiplied easily and simply. They are appearing in the physical at every moment, in direct relation to whatever you are focusing on. However, because it is "Law" that we are working with, "Whatever you ask is what you are getting." Recognize the fact that your thoughts, words, and actions are the basis to what you create and experience in your life. There is no greater truth.

✓ **Parable of the Man Who Sowed Good Seed Into the Ground – Jesus speaking to multitude and disciples**

In this section we are directed to allow, nurture, and focus on the good as it grows within us, in the midst of what we would call our personal shortcomings.

Matthew 13:24-30

24Another parable put he forth unto them, saying, The kingdom of heaven is likened unto a man which sowed good seed in his field:

25But while men slept, his enemy came and sowed tares among the wheat, and went his way.

26But when the blade was sprung up, and brought forth fruit, then appeared the tares also.

27So the servants of the householder came and said unto him, Sir, didst not thou sow good seed in thy field? from whence then hath it tares?

28He said unto them, An enemy hath done this. The servants said unto him, Wilt thou then that we go and gather them up?
29But he said, Nay; lest while ye gather up the tares, ye root up also the wheat with them.

30Let both grow together until the harvest: and in the time of harvest I will say to the reapers, Gather ye together first the tares, and bind them in bundles to burn them: but gather the wheat into my barn.

Mark 4:26-29

26And he said, So is the kingdom of God, as if a man should cast seed into the ground;

²⁷And should sleep, and rise night and day, and the seed should spring and grow up, he knoweth not how.

²⁸For the earth bringeth forth fruit of herself; first the blade, then the ear, after that the full corn in the ear.

²⁹But when the fruit is brought forth, immediately he putteth in the sickle, because the harvest is come.

This parable likens the "Kingdom of Heaven", the "Kingdom of God", to a man who sowed good seed into the ground, or in his field. Good seed has been sewn by God all around the world, and the world's field is vast and wide. The question is no longer when or where the seed is sewn, it is whether we will allow the seed to grow. We as a global society have become numb, because of misunderstanding, that many scriptures require only literal interpretation. Meaning, all scriptures explain that to realize God, to truly know God, you must control the mind, the emotions, and your thoughts. This is uniform. The seed has been sewn in the form of the scriptures of the world. It is up to us, each individual, to prepare the ground of our heart, and allow those words to grow, create in us a new nature, the appropriate nature for the "Kingdom of God" to work through us and for your life and the world around us to become an out-picturing of the "Kingdom of God", the beauty inside of us.

✓ **Parable of the Mustard Seed – Jesus speaking to multitude and disciples**

In this section we observe that the "Kingdom", once sewn inside the individual, grows until its beauty and magnificence begins to out-picture into the person's life experience.

Mathew 13:31-32

31Another parable put he forth unto them, saying, The kingdom of heaven is like to a grain of mustard seed, which a man took, and sowed in his field:

32Which indeed is the least of all seeds: but when it is grown, it is the greatest among herbs, and becometh a tree, so that the birds of the air come and lodge in the branches thereof.

Mark 4: 30-32

30And he said, Whereunto shall we liken the kingdom of God? or with what comparison shall we compare it?

31It is like a grain of mustard seed, which, when it is sown in the earth, is less than all the seeds that be in the earth:

32But when it is sown, it groweth up, and becometh greater than all herbs, and shooteth out great branches; so that the fowls of the air may lodge under the shadow of it.

Luke 13: 18-19

18Then said he, Unto what is the kingdom of God like? and whereunto shall I resemble it?

19It is like a grain of mustard seed, which a man took, and cast into his garden; and it grew, and waxed a great tree; and the fowls of the air lodged in the branches of it.

The "Kingdom of God" is compared to a mustard seed, for the mustard seed is one of the smallest seeds, and the "Kingdom of God" resides in the unseen, is the least obvious, is the most overlooked, therefore is the most insignificant, and is taken the least seriously. However, just as the mustard seed grows into a great tree in which birds can lodge, so does the "Kingdom of God and the Love Unconditional". As it grows and matures in you, it becomes a grand, magnificent source of strength, conviction, determination, and its basis of Unconditional Love overtakes people, circumstances, and events of the material nature, while you move toward that of your choosing. The immense strength of the "Kingdom", of Love cannot be denied. I remind you of recent times and what Gandhi did with the power of Love and nonviolence in his country, and the ending of slavery in the United States. It was not the hate of a people that ended slavery; it was the Love of a people.

✓ **Parable of Leaven – Jesus speaking to multitude and the disciples**

In this section we observe that the "Kingdom", once inside, pushes the individual to grow, to expand their current way of thinking, speaking, and acting.

Matthew 13:33

³³Another parable spake he unto them; The kingdom of heaven is like unto leaven, which a woman took, and hid in three measures of meal, till the whole was leavened.

Luke 13:20-21

²⁰And again he said, Whereunto shall I liken the kingdom of God?

²¹It is like leaven, which a woman took and hid in three measures of meal, till the whole was leavened.

This parable likens the "Kingdom of God" to leaven—or yeast—used to make the flour dough rise. The "Kingdom of Heaven", once you begin allowing the seeds to grow within you, develops, spreads, and becomes a part of your entire being. This development must be protected from the normal way of life, and must be cultivated continuously to preserve it from unwanted weeds or choking vines. Prayer is called for. Meditation is called for. Turning off the TV's and radios is called for, so that the cultivation of the spirit of the scriptures, the spirit of God, "Unconditional Love", is not contaminated by thoughts, behaviors and ideas which are contradictory to "Unconditional Love." This requires great discipline and will set you against many habits that are currently yours, but, then again, what did you think it meant to "Take up your cross", or "To deny yourself"?

70

✓ **Parable of Treasure Hid in a Field – Jesus speaking to the disciples**

In this section we observe that the "Kingdom", once found, must become the most important thing for it to become prevalent and evident in a person's life.

Matthew 13:44

⁴⁴Again, the kingdom of heaven is like unto treasure hid in a field; the which when a man hath found, he hideth, and for joy thereof goeth and selleth all that he hath, and buyeth that field.

This parable likens the "Kingdom of God" to a treasure that is hidden in a field, which, once found, is hidden. The finder then sells all that he has and purchases the field. The "Kingdom of Heaven" is a treasure, a wonderful treasure. However, we must simply believe, until we realize or recognize that we are experiencing the results of abiding by the "Kingdom" which we have placed in our hearts, our inner most being. This scripture states that upon finding, one hides it, and for joy, goes and sells all that he has and buys the field. This is indicative of a change in focus. Once you find the "Kingdom", begin to cultivate it in your heart, and begin to see its out-picturing or results in all that you do, you make it your sole focus.

✓ **Parable of the Merchant Seeking Pearls – Jesus speaking to disciples**

In this section we observe that the "Kingdom", once found, is and should be the most important, the most valuable thing to a person.

Matthew 13:45-46

⁴⁵Again, the kingdom of heaven is like unto a merchant man, seeking goodly pearls:

⁴⁶Who, when he had found one pearl of great price, went and sold all that he had, and bought it.

This parable likens the "Kingdom of Heaven", to a merchant seeking pearls. Every honest person will admit that he is searching. People are always on a quest for true happiness. They are searching for true Love. They are searching for the means to live comfortably and to provide for their families without worry or care. We are all searching for our pearls. Some of the pearls are the same, yet many are different, and there is nothing wrong with any of the pearls they are seeking. However, the pearl of the "Kingdom", of "Unconditional Love", once found and allowed to grow within, is realized to be the most valuable pearl of all. Once this is realized, one will go and sell all he has, or change his focus, from the other pearls to the one of greatest value, not knowing that the result of nourishing, cultivating, and polishing this single pearl to perfection provides all the necessary tools, and then some, to find all the other pearls without worry, or care of opposition.

✓ **Parable of Net Cast Into the Sea That Gathers Up Every Kind – Jesus speaking to disciples**

In this section we observe that the "Kingdom" accepts all, however, the bad are those who refuse to accept the challenge of LOVE and personal responsibility in their lives.

Matthew 13:47-50

⁴⁷Again, the kingdom of heaven is like unto a net, that was cast into the sea, and gathered of every kind:

⁴⁸Which, when it was full, they drew to shore, and sat down, and gathered the good into vessels, but cast the bad away.

⁴⁹So shall it be at the end of the world: the angels shall come forth, and sever the wicked from among the just,

⁵⁰And shall cast them into the furnace of fire: there shall be wailing and gnashing of teeth.

This parable likens the "Kingdom of God" to a net cast into the sea that gathers up every kind. The "Kingdom of Heaven", the "Kingdom of God" is everywhere all at once, and partakes of each of us as we allow it. Those who partake of the "Kingdom" and have it inside of them are the good. Those who are without the "Kingdom" are cast aside by "Law", and are subject to the pain and suffering of this world. The abundance of LOVE or the lack thereof, is the path the individual has chosen. No two paths can be walked at the same time.

Summary:

The "Kingdom of God", the "The Kingdom of Heaven", is the most misunderstood, misrepresented location in the history of mankind. Too often, the many scholars and theologians, who seem to be learned and educated have only taken the descriptions and perceptions of those who have come before them to heart, and created a whole dramatized version of the teachings of the most recognized and most significant character in the Bible. However, if you study the teachings of Jesus directly, independently, with a blank slate, and add to that blank slate the teachings of the other major scriptures of the world, you will see that they sing in unison that the "Kingdom of Heaven", our point of contact with the Source of all creation, is deep, deep inside of each of us. It is beyond the inner most parts of our being, located far into the unfathomable, the unthinkable, and the inconceivable. There, with much work, much practice, and much perseverance can one reach unison, oneness with the Source of all, which many have done, in our world's past, and who are living presently. The question that remains is that if this is true, how did the perception of words that lie on the pages, in plain sight, become twisted to the point where one can read and not see, listen and not hear. It is simple; we, as individuals, have not put forth the work necessary to experience for ourselves. Even though most denominations of Christianity do not openly say that you must go through the pastor or any one in position to reach God, this teaching still remains, implied, and has most people only believing what is spoken to them from a pulpit, rather than searching and finding out through experience for themselves. Spiritual growth is an individual path. You do not get points for communing with a large group of people. You only grow as your faith and trust grow, and these only grow as you experience the truth of Unconditional Love in your life, and how it changes the results of situations that would not have normally turned out your way. When will you have dominion over your life? When will the gates of your life begin to open and allow true happiness and success in, or do things fall apart for you every time the light begins to peek through? If you are not experiencing what you feel is your truth, you have not found the "Kingdom", and until you believe and exercise the fact that the Source of all that you are and all that you need is located within you, you will continue to suffer with no way out. The choice is yours. Forgiveness is yours. Change your perception. This is your life. See if you realize a power surge of your soul and spirit as they shift your life out of neutral and into drive for the first time.

Chapter III

God's Love – Unconditional (Law)

At what point can we stop being LOVE Unconditional?

Matthew 5:39-47 – Jesus Speaking to Disciples

39But I say unto you, That ye resist not evil: but whosoever shall smite thee on thy right cheek, turn to him the other also.

40And if any man will sue thee at the law, and take away thy coat, let him have thy cloak also.

41And whosoever shall compel thee to go a mile, go with him twain.

42Give to him that asketh thee, and from him that would borrow of thee turn not thou away.

43Ye have heard that it hath been said, Thou shalt love thy neighbour, and hate thine enemy.

44But I say unto you, Love your enemies, bless them that curse you, do good to them that hate you, and pray for them which despitefully use you, and persecute you;

45That ye may be the children of your Father which is in heaven: for he maketh his sun to rise on the evil and on the good, and sendeth rain on the just and on the unjust.

46For if ye love them which love you, what reward have ye? do not even the publicans the same?

47And if ye salute your brethren only, what do ye more than others? do not even the publicans so?

The tremors inside each and everyone shake us to the core when we are confronted with behaviors, situations, or circumstances that we know are less than God, because they perplex us, they jar our system. The spirit mind and the body of man, for an instant, say no, and then succumb to the path each of us has taken. If we have committed offence, often we are regretful or feel guilty within ourselves. We then need to forgive ourselves for the behavior which we have just demonstrated, and that went contradictory to the wish of our soul. If we were offended, often the mind and emotions jump into autopilot and behave in ways that are parallel or consistent with the behaviors of those around us. This is never the way of Unconditional Love.

Resist not evil means not to push against or reject those feelings or behaviors which are your normal way of being or acting. Trust is the first level of business, for you must recognize that you have within you the ability to perform at a higher level, to behave on a higher plane, and to respond to people, situations, and circumstances from a higher position. Communicate with those who offend. Every one who offends has been offended. Notice the inner turmoil when you have been hurt, the hurt that you feel is the result of an exterior event triggering something that is unresolved inside you. Otherwise, you would not have taken offence. The strength to remain balanced and at peace no matter what, is a grand position of power. Yet, to reach it, requires discipline and perseverance in dealing with your self. The outer, exterior world only brings to your attention what work needs to be done inside you for the necessary growth to occur. Does this sound unreasonable? Does this sound unkind? It is however, necessary. It is that which provides the ground work for the Universal Force of life to begin making its presence known in and through you. This life force, this presence, God, has no individual respect. God has no favorites, God makes no choices. God just is, and we are in this life governed by Law, not by chance and not by decree. God sends rain on the just and the unjust. The sun rises on the good and the not so good. So, if God presents us all with equal Love, with equal beauty, with equal opportunity, what is the deciding factor? It is our personal choice. It is the choice to walk in the light or not. It is in loving unconditionally or not, and the Law is that whatever you are "Being", whatever you are choosing to believe about you, whatever you are choosing to think, speak, and act upon in your life. Ultimately, it is what you experience. This is Law, this is the choice. You can choose and change at any time.

Being and acting from Unconditional LOVE, aligns you, and connects you with the "Kingdom", and the treasures you acquire are rewarded you in this physical life.

Matthew 6:19-21 – Jesus Speaking to Disciples

¹⁹Lay not up for yourselves treasures upon earth, where moth and rust doth corrupt, and where thieves break through and steal:

²⁰But lay up for yourselves treasures in heaven, where neither moth nor rust doth corrupt, and where thieves do not break through nor steal

²¹For where your treasure is, there will your heart be also.

The treasures that you seek are not the treasures of the utmost high. To know what you are seeking, you only have to look to what you are getting. This is where your focus is, plain and simple. The "Kingdom of God" is a realm of abundance, a realm of health, a realm of harmony and peace, and unless you are focused on "Being" these things instead of "acquiring" these things, you will never have them. You can never get what you already have; you can never become something you already are. By focusing on the Love of God "Unconditional", and allowing it to flow and grow in and through you, you begin to become aware of all the powerful qualities that reside within you, that have been suppressed by fear and disbelief. The Love of God is all consuming, and also all revealing. In order to realize it in you, you must first confront yourself. You must confront all that you are, and all that you think you know, and come to realize that we really don't know anything. You need to realize that God, the Universal Life Source is nothing and everything, all at the same time, and that the only way to know who we truly are is to surrender all understanding and knowledge to God, your friend, saying, "This is me, with a blank slate, your friend." Thus, allowing God, to lay at your feet the greatest treasure that you could ever claim for yourself. This one treasure allows God to provide you with all that you will ever need to achieve in this life and to have whatever you desire, with the good graces of the all, for they will be byproducts, unknowing beneficiaries of the union, your connection with God the Source. Your focus is the key. Be a friend to God, a loved one. Stop seeking the hand of God and begin to seek God's face. This is the path of the spiritually mature. This is the path of purpose. This is your path of power.

Who can ask, and what should you expect from God the Source?
Luke 11:5-13 – Jesus Speaking to Disciples

⁵ And he said unto them, Which of you shall have a friend, and shall go unto him at midnight, and say unto him, Friend, lend me three loaves;

⁶ For a friend of mine in his journey is come to me, and I have nothing to set before him?

⁷ And he from within shall answer and say, Trouble me not: the door is now shut, and my children are with me in bed; I cannot rise and give thee.

⁸ I say unto you, Though he will not rise and give him, because he is his friend, yet because of his importunity he will rise and give him as many as he needeth.

⁹ And I say unto you, Ask, and it shall be given you; seek, and ye shall find; knock, and it shall be opened unto you.

¹⁰For every one that asketh receiveth; and he that seeketh findeth; and to him that knocketh it shall be opened.

¹¹If a son shall ask bread of any of you that is a father, will he give him a stone? or if he ask a fish, will he for a fish give him a serpent?

¹²Or if he shall ask an egg, will he offer him a scorpion?

¹³If ye then, being evil, know how to give good gifts unto your children: how much more shall your heavenly Father give the Holy Spirit to them that ask him?

The LOVE of God the Source must be compared to that which we know in human experience, for it is very difficult to imagine Unconditional Love from a human perspective, until you actually begin to grow in it to see what it is capable of. Here, it is likened to a friend of a friend who is interrupted late at night and basically asked for a favor, and because of persistence responds to your summons. God's Love is also likened to that of a father, who, not truly knowing God or true LOVE, would still never give to his child anything detrimental when it has specific needs and has asked for what it needs exactly and directly.

Come to know the fact that the Love, which we call Love as humans, has nothing to do with the LOVE of God. We can only do our best to describe and intellectually explain the LOVE of God as it relates to our material experience until we actually experience it in our innermost being. When that

happens we are faced with another dilemma. Because we are limited to our words, it becomes difficult to describe or explain what that true LOVE feels like. Exhilarating, overwhelming, quenching through and through comes to mind. It does not care who you are. It does not care what you have or have not done. It does not care where you came from. It does not care where you are going. It does not care what you did last night. It does not remember as humans do. It does not feel as humans do. It "Simply Is" and that's all it is. Behind the confusion that has been amassed in each of our minds that's all it is, and at some point, while we do the necessary work, each of us as individuals will realize the truth of it. Unconditional Love does not try to control a spouse or a loved one. Unconditional Love does not judge or condemn. Unconditional Love allows that which is to be, until it is ready to do more or be more, and it continues to support that which is, where ever it is, no matter what. Unconditional Love gives and gives and gives, endlessly. Unconditional Love always seeks to understand, never to command or impose guilt. Unconditional Love is also fiercely direct with truth, for the truth pierces to the Soul. Anything that is changing is not Truth. Truth is Universal; it is not limited to anyone or anything. Unconditional Love is giving and supporting without requiring or expecting. Unconditional Love is LOVE unconditional.

Appearances can be deceiving?

Luke 13:30

30And, behold, there are last which shall be first, and there are first which shall be last.

To place a rank or position on someone when it comes to the "Kingdom of God" is difficult because when it comes to spiritual things there is no rank and order as in the military. There is simply you, the individual, and where you are and what you have come to understand, live and experience.

81

Turmoil in a life indicates the level of growth. Fear in words, actions, and behaviors indicate levels of growth. The position or current relationship that a person claims to have with God the Source is indicative of their level of growth. Are they lucky to be here and to get the scraps from the table of God? Are they tossed back and forth by life and thankful that God is allowing them to suffer for whatever reason? Or, are they sitting at the table planning their next move, with God, so that the Source of all can make itself known through them into this physical world, providing grand service to all that they are meant to touch? Which one are you? One is a weak disgrace if you claim to be a "Child of God", and one is approaching dominion. One is the person in the scriptures with five talents who multiplied, and the other is the person who was given one talent, who went and hid, fearful and shameful (Matthew 25:14-30).

The rewards that you receive for your work will be apparent in your life. There are and will be many who appear to be first, who appear to be chosen, who appear to be knowledgeable and special in the eyes of the Kingdom, but you simply have to spend enough time to see who they truly are. Is their life truly evident of what they appear to portray? Are they working toward what they speak of, or are they simply telling you to do it. There is a difference in hearing and applying. There is a difference in believing and knowing. Love makes itself known, makes its presence apparent. Everything less than Love makes itself known as well. We have all seen what that looks like.

Summary:

Unconditional Love. It is difficult to explain or even fathom Unconditional Love, for we cannot look at it from a human or physical point of view. First, it is not the Love we associate with any of our emotions. Anything associated with our emotions is only there because of a need that is being met or is not being met. This is the cause of much of the turmoil within relationships that so many say is love. Really, normally, there are two people who were attracted to, and connected with each other because they each filled an emotional void which could not be met any other way. For instance, I want to feel appreciated and my partner shows me appreciation. I feel as though I need to be the center of attention, and my partner shows me that level of attention. I want to feel secure financially and be taken care of, and my partner does that. In the current makeup of most relationships each partner fills a void in the other person, either consciously or unconsciously, and many of these voids are created during childhood and along the way in life, and when we meet that person we call it love. The problem with this is that as soon as one of the partners stops filling the void or becomes unable to fill the void, we say we have fallen out of love, because our needs are no longer met. This was never Love in the first place; this was two individuals with emotional deficiencies filling each other's voids. True relationship is where two or more individuals come together, who are happy with themselves as individuals, who Love themselves first, who do not need any one else to show them Love or attention to fill any emotional void because they have realized that everything they need already lies within them, and they have recognized it, grown it, and are now in position to GIVE what they have to others. In a 'loving' relationship, the partners have the opportunity to define themselves to the greatest extent, while defining who they choose to be and what they choose to give or how they choose to serve others through that relationship. Yes, this has nothing to do with trying to judge a partner, mate or friend. This has nothing to do with trying to control a partner, mate or friend. This has nothing to with having or trying to make another be or become something that they are not or is not of their own choosing.

As you can see, Unconditional Love requires great strength, inner strength, and it can be developed just like a muscle. It must be developed in order to understand the nature of God the Source. Unconditional Love does not judge, at all. Individuals do what they do, based on where they are in their growth, and because of the life and the world they perceive to be true for them at the time. There is no right or wrong, it just is, and the more we try to impose our thoughts or understandings on others or tell them they are wrong, the more we create disturbance in our selves and in others. Unconditional Love does not judge. Unconditional Love is compassionate and understanding. Unconditional Love is compassionate and understanding to the prostitute who is doing what they feel they need to do to support their family, or just to support themselves, and sees no other way. Is any situation or circumstance wrong when the individual mind of a man or woman cannot see any other option? It does not matter if you can see it or not. Unconditional Love is universal. It does not care who you are, what color, what shape, where you are located, whether you are angry today or excited. The strength of Unconditional Love knows that the physical makeup and the emotions of the moment are only a blanket, a temporary covering of the true you. Unconditional Love recognizes and sees the magnificence that resides within you and treats you accordingly, whether you recognize it yet or not. Unconditional Love is true. Unconditional Love understands that silence is often stronger than words, and that directness, when appropriate, is a powerful tool for change. The job to move into this position is each individual's choice. The responsibility to move into this position is each individual's choice. This is a prerequisite to allowing God the Source to work through you, and for you to really get to know God. Get out of the mind of man. Come to the absolute realization that you do not 'know', and open yourself up to infinite knowledge, being grateful for everything. Know that people act according to their level of growth and LOVE them anyway. LOVE them anyway. LOVE them anyway. If you cannot, the problem is not with them, it is with you.

Chapter IV

Get To The Point!

✓ **Personal Responsibility**

Jesus tells the disciples that he WILL NOT increase our faith. We are each charged with the "Personal Responsibility" of bearing our own cross. The "CHOICE" of Unconditional Love, or not, is an individual choice.

Luke 17:1-10 – Jesus Speaking to Disciples

¹ Then said he unto the disciples, It is impossible but that offences will come: but woe unto him, through whom they come!

² It were better for him that a millstone were hanged about his neck, and he cast into the sea, than that he should offend one of these little ones.

³ Take heed to yourselves: If thy brother trespass against thee, rebuke him; and if he repent, forgive him.

⁴ And if he trespass against thee seven times in a day, and seven times in a day turn again to thee, saying, I repent; thou shalt forgive him.

⁵ And the apostles said unto the Lord, Increase our faith.

⁶ And the Lord said, If ye had faith as a grain of mustard seed, ye might say unto this sycamine tree, Be thou plucked up by the root, and be thou planted in the sea; and it should obey you.

7 But which of you, having a servant plowing or feeding cattle, will say unto him by and by, when he is come from the field, Go and sit down to meat?

8 And will not rather say unto him, Make ready wherewith I may sup, and gird thyself, and serve me, till I have eaten and drunken; and afterward thou shalt eat and drink?

9 Doth he thank that servant because he did the things that were commanded him? I trow not.

10So likewise ye, when ye shall have done all those things which are commanded you, say, We are unprofitable servants: we have done that which was our duty to do.

Grand is the choice to take "Personal Responsibility" in your life. The above scripture, spoken from Jesus, is an interesting thing. How and why would he say that? Could he have said that? It does not equate to anything that I have been taught or that I hear on a regular basis. The norm is that Jesus will bless, that we are allowed what we have through Jesus, and Jesus died for our salvation so that we might be saved. These are the current teachings amid the masses. However, it directly contradicts the statements made by Jesus himself. Basically, Jesus is saying that he will not increase our faith, he will not do anything that it is commanded that we must do for ourselves. He equates his disciples and all people with the servant who has worked in the field and then comes in to sit down or to fix dinner. It is not okay to congratulate a person for doing what they are supposed to do, and Jesus is saying that the increasing or growing in faith is *our responsibility*. His teachings are the roadmap to salvation, to the rising above of the pain and suffering of this world, this physical experience, but it is up to us to follow, to do, and to apply the teachings. Presently, and sadly, the masses are content to believe that all they are, that all they have or do not have, whether desired or not, is depended upon someone or something that is separate from themselves, separate from the individual. This is not true. Given the power

of choice, each of us, at any given moment, can begin to apply the "Teachings of Christ" and begin to experience what a change, an alteration of the dimensions of the makeup of our nature will have on the outer experiences that we have in life. Jesus spoke these words, and many others that support this scripture whole heartedly. The question is will you continue to allow yourself to be blind to scriptures that have been there all along? Scriptures that have obviously been allowed to lie dormant, for they will alter the whole of the teachings that the masses have accepted for so long. The time has come to discover just how far we can go in taking "Personal Responsibility" for our lives. It is two completely different things to say that God is working on us, and doing to us, versus saying and knowing that God wants to work through us. Study for yourself. Open your eyes. Return to the fresh mindset of a child, untainted, uncontaminated by confused misunderstood teachings, and see what happens when you apply under the mindset of "That is what it says." It does not matter whether you believe it or not. It just is.

✓ **The "Kingdom of God", the "Kingdom of Heaven"**

The "Kingdom of God", is located deep within you. It is beyond the body, it is beyond the soul, it is beyond your spirit and the spirit in which it resides. The choice to allow your connection to germinate and grow is available every second, every moment, but it is up to you to cultivate it.

Matthew 24:26 – Jesus Speaking to Disciples

26Wherefore if they shall say unto you, Behold, he is in the desert; go not forth: behold, he is in the secret chambers; believe it not.

John 4:13-14 – Jesus Speaking to Samaritan Woman at the Well

13Jesus answered and said unto her, Whosoever drinketh of this water shall thirst again:

14But whosoever drinketh of the water that I shall give him shall never thirst; but the water that I shall give him shall be in him a well of water springing up into everlasting life.

Luke 17:20-21

20And when he was demanded of the Pharisees, when the kingdom of God should come, he answered them and said, The kingdom of God cometh not with observation:

21Neither shall they say, Lo here! or, lo there! for, behold, the kingdom of God is within you.

John 7:38 – Jesus Speaking to Jews

38He that believeth on me, as the scripture hath said, out of his belly shall flow rivers of living water.

So You Call Yourself A Christian?

The "Kingdom of Heaven"; I cannot iterate this enough. To locate the truth for yourself, to find the missing link to all that you think you can be and know that you should be, you merely have to be quiet, be still, and ask who you truly are, and God will answer. The lies will fall away. The contradictions will fall away, and the answers will ring real and true to you. The seeds of the words, the teachings, of Jesus, if truly allowed to germinate inside of you will grow and blossom into magnificence indescribable. It will grow into a presence, a force, spewing up from inside you and into the world with a quiet beauty and power realized by you and felt by everyone. It is within your grasp, it has always been within you, you just have never delved deep enough. You have never risked opening up enough. You have never trusted yourself enough, but I am telling you that if you begin to remove the clouds of everything that is less than LOVE in your life and in your mind, your thoughts, words, and actions, you will find the joy that you seek; you will find the peace that you seek, you will find the strength that you seek, for an infinite supply is yours. It always has been. Many of the Bible scriptures support this fact, however, the teachings to the masses are fraught with many implied messages that the mind becomes blind to what is right in front of the eyes. Open yourself to truth, to the grandest possibilities for you and your life. Open yourself to the scriptures and the words which lay directly in front of you, and that support the possibilities without limitations in your life. Scrap those teachings which slam the door to all that you could achieve in your life. God is infinite, therefore you are. There are no limits to the possibilities of God; therefore there are no limits to your possibilities. Let the seeds of Jesus' teachings truly grow from the inside out, and see that where you thought there was weakness, there is strength. See that where you thought there was death, there is life. See that God is quietly watching your world and your life through your eyes with you, and is waiting for you to turn up the heat on the approach to your goals and dreams. Consistently work to

90

become true. Consistently work to Love Unconditionally, and see what power has always been there, inside, for you to wield.

✓ Our Position According To Jesus

Who are you serving? I don't understand!

John 15:14-16 – Jesus Speaking to Disciples

¹⁴Ye are my friends, if ye do whatsoever I command you.

¹⁵Henceforth I call you not servants; for the servant knoweth not what his lord doeth: but I have called you friends; for all things that I have heard of my Father I have made known unto you.

¹⁶Ye have not chosen me, but I have chosen you, and ordained you, that ye should go and bring forth fruit, and that your fruit should remain: that whatsoever ye shall ask of the Father in my name, he may give it you.

"I am your lowly, humble servant."
"I am not worthy of you or your blessings."
Have you ever heard these sayings? These are a disgrace and an embarrassment to Jesus and to God the Source. Plainly and obviously Jesus said that if we keep his sayings, or his commandments, we are his friends and not his servants. Do you see that? So where did all the horrible not worthy, less than stuff come from? Think about it. The trees bloom fully and beautifully on their own, exactly and perfectly when they are supposed to. The flowers bloom gloriously and magnificently exactly and perfectly when they are supposed to. So how can the glory and magnificence of nature and all of its abundance, created by God the Source be, and cannot be contained in the statement "Wow!" Yet, somehow from all of that, we, supposedly God's highest creation, call ourselves the lowest, the least worthy of care, love, and abundance in all forms. Who started this lie, for Jesus never said this, but man has allowed it to grow and grow to the point where we do not

even see the words on the pages of the scriptures that we study. A friend walks side by side with you. A friend does not walk behind or in front. A friend shares everything that he knows and everything that he has, so that you may be able to do, accomplish, have, and be in the same position, of the same rank and status as he is. A friend helps or assists you when you need it, but does *not do it for you* because a true friend knows to do something for you, deprives you of strength and growth. Jesus makes it plain that he is a friend to all who keep his teachings. He is a brother to all in God's family. We are the son whose father was overjoyed at his return. We are the sheep whose shepherd leaves the flock to go and search for the one. You are valuable. You are worthy, and to claim or accept teachings that imply that you are anything less than a friend to Jesus and a child of God the Source is a lie, and that lie will hold you down in weakness and misery, while God continues to send you Goals and Dreams which appear out of your reach because the lie you believe and clouds your vision. Either you believe what Jesus said or you don't. Either you work from a position of strength or you don't. Either you allow LOVE to be your guide, OR YOU DON'T.

✓ **I Can Do What?**

The things I did, you will do also, and more!!!
John 14:12, 15, 17 – Jesus Speaking to Disciples

[12]Verily, verily, I say unto you, He that believeth on me, the works that I do shall he do also; and greater works than these shall he do; because I go unto my Father.

[15]If ye love me, keep my commandments.

[17]Even the Spirit of truth; whom the world cannot receive, because it seeth him not, neither knoweth him: but ye know him; for he dwelleth with you, and shall be in you.

Yes, you can do it, too, if you only believe. This is the epitome of the scriptures misunderstood, least talked about, least preached about, and least discussed, because if you get to the Truth of this single passage of scripture it changes the dynamics of how the "Teachings of Jesus" are being taught to the masses. Here Jesus is telling the disciples and us that we are capable of doing all of the works that he did, and that we will do even more. Think about it. Read it again. Do not ask anyone else what they think, only look deep within yourself, try to reach beyond the fears, try to see beyond the doubts, and ask YOURSELF if it could possibly be true for you.

If it is true it means that God has been with you all along. It means that God's power has been your power all along. If it is true it means that you have struggled in your life not by choice, not by God's will, but because of misunderstanding; and that kinda burns me up. The words have been on the page for generations and generations, but the mind has been trained, well trained, in disbelief, worry, and doubt, which is the same challenge that Jesus faced in his day, with his own personal disciples. So now, think about how the perception of the message, the "Teachings", of Jesus has been melted, watered down to the point where we do not even see words as they are written on the pages. The masses have chosen simply to follow and flounder aimlessly in life, while being beaten up and smashed against the rocks of misunderstanding and ignorance, but now you have the chance to start a new. Create a fresh slate, look at your life to this point. If your current beliefs and understandings are not leading you to dominion over your life, begin to see the same scriptures through new eyes, from a new perspective. Would Jesus be proud of your current efforts and results, or would he not know you at all?

✓ **The Goal**

Perfection

"Perfection is the goal." Nobody is perfect, or can this be a lie? Matthew 5:48 – Jesus to Disciples

48Be ye therefore perfect, even as your Father which is in heaven is perfect.

Luke 6:40

40The disciple is not above his master: but every one that is perfect shall be as his master.

The perfection of the Soul and the Spirit is just that, Perfect. The only place where confusion lies is in the mind. This is where the clouds are, the mist, the fog. This is where control has been lost. This is where all sheep of God the Source go astray. This is where the masses give up the reigns of their own life to the words and beliefs of others. Worthy of your life, they are not. Worthy of your trust, they are not. Worthy of your children, they are not, for the mind of man must be protected. The garden of your mind must be constantly cultivated and groomed. The weeds that are constantly infiltrating your mind must be pulled and discarded on a daily basis so that the seeds of Love can be allowed to grow and blossom fully. The seeds of truth must be continuously sewn and watered, fed and observed working in your life, so that the roots can grow deep and spread wide. Is perfection attainable? Yes. Can perfection be yours? Yes. Jesus said so himself. Where did the saying come from that no one is perfect, that I am not perfect? It is a lie, and a cop-out for the work that should be going on. Perfection is your birth right as well. Freedom is your birthright as well. It all resides in your spirit, you simply need to believe the words that lie in front of you in the scriptures, and begin to allow the Light, Perfection, to flow through you into your physical being and experience. There is power there. There is courage there. The LOVE you seek is there, and it is yours. The happiness you seek is there, and it is yours. The passion and zeal for life, no matter what, is there, and it is yours. Either you believe the scriptures or you do not. From this point on, either you choose to listen and believe teachings that keep you in a weakened state, or you choose to break free from the path of the masses. I remind you that this has never, all through history, ever, ever, ever, been the right path. Never has what everyone been doing been the right path. It has always been the path of least resistance, and there are always disastrous consequences to face at the other end. I beg you to turn away, make a u-turn, and switch lanes onto the path, which, if you look closely and feel deeply, is all Power and Perfection. This is your choice, as of Now. You can choose. Right now. Make a decision to begin to explore your self. Find out how to work your way back to perfection. It was yours when you entered this world, but now you can return to it, and learn how to trust it and wield it consciously with God the Source at your side. Perfection is your goal, find your way back. Jesus said the path is narrow, the gate is strait, and few will find it. If few will find it, there is no way that, if you are doing what everyone else is doing, you are on the right path. If you have dreams but do not know where to start, you have not found it. If you have doubts and cannot release them, you have not found it. If you are not at peace on the inside you have not found it. If you do not believe that you can achieve perfection you will never find it, because you have cut yourself off from it with disbelief. What do you choose? This has always been the dilemma of the human being.

So You Call Yourself A Christian?

Oneness

Spiritual Oneness is the topic. *Every single thing* emanates from God the Source. This means that the Source of all is in us, we are in it, and we are in each other, because in essence, at the most fundamental level, we are all one. With this being said, what you do unto your neighbor, at the most fundamental level, you are doing to yourself. This is what he is saying.

Matthew 22:39 – Jesus Speaking of Second Greatest Commandment

³⁹And the second is like unto it, Thou shalt love thy neighbour as thyself.

Matthew 25:31-46 – Jesus Speaking to Disciples

³¹When the Son of man shall come in his glory, and all the holy angels with him, then shall he sit upon the throne of his glory:

³²And before him shall be gathered all nations: and he shall separate them one from another, as a shepherd divideth his sheep from the goats:

³³And he shall set the sheep on his right hand, but the goats on the left.

³⁴Then shall the King say unto them on his right hand, Come, ye blessed of my Father, inherit the kingdom prepared for you from the foundation of the world:

³⁵For I was an hungred, and ye gave me meat: I was thirsty, and ye gave me drink: I was a stranger, and ye took me in:

³⁶Naked, and ye clothed me: I was sick, and ye visited me: I was in prison, and ye came unto me.

37Then shall the righteous answer him, saying, Lord, when saw we thee an hungred, and fed thee? or thirsty, and gave thee drink?

38When saw we thee a stranger, and took thee in? or naked, and clothed thee?

39Or when saw we thee sick, or in prison, and came unto thee?

40And the King shall answer and say unto them, Verily I say unto you, Inasmuch as ye have done it unto one of the least of these my brethren, ye have done it unto me.

41Then shall he say also unto them on the left hand, Depart from me, ye cursed, into everlasting fire, prepared for the devil and his angels:

42For I was an hungred, and ye gave me no meat: I was thirsty, and ye gave me no drink:

43I was a stranger, and ye took me not in: naked, and ye clothed me not: sick, and in prison, and ye visited me not.

44Then shall they also answer him, saying, Lord, when saw we thee an hungred, or athirst, or a stranger, or naked, or sick, or in prison, and did not minister unto thee?

45Then shall he answer them, saying, Verily I say unto you, Inasmuch as ye did it not to one of the least of these, ye did it not to me.

46And these shall go away into everlasting punishment: but the righteous into life eternal.

Mark 9:37 – Jesus Speaking to Disciples

37Whosoever shall receive one of such children in my name, receiveth me: and whosoever shall receive me, receiveth not me, but him that sent me.

So You Call Yourself A Christian?

Mark 12:31-34 – Jesus Speaking to the Scribe

[31]And the second is like, namely this, Thou shalt love thy neighbour as thyself. There is none other commandment greater than these.

[32]And the scribe said unto him, Well, Master, thou hast said the truth: for there is one God; and there is none other but he:

[33]And to love him with all the heart, and with all the understanding, and with all the soul, and with all the strength, and to love his neighbour as himself, is more than all whole burnt offerings and sacrifices.

[34]And when Jesus saw that he answered discreetly, he said unto him, Thou art not far from the kingdom of God. And no man after that durst ask him any question.

Luke 9:48 – Jesus Speaking to Disciples

[48]And said unto them, Whosoever shall receive this child in my name receiveth me: and whosoever shall receive me receiveth him that sent me: for he that is least among you all, the same shall be great.

John 14:20 – Jesus Speaking to Disciples

[20]At that day ye shall know that I am in my Father, and ye in me, and I in you.

John 17:22-23 – Jesus Speaking to God

[20]Neither pray I for these alone, but for them also which shall believe on me through their word;

[21]That they all may be one; as thou, Father, art in me, and I in thee, that they also may be one in us: that the world may believe that thou hast sent me.

[22]And the glory which thou gavest me I have given them; that they may be one, even as we are one:

²³I in them, and thou in me, that they may be made perfect in one; and that the world may know that thou hast sent me, and hast loved them, as thou hast loved me.

Oneness is the fundamental principle that is forgotten and overlooked because of how it changes the game, and causes contradiction in the way the scriptures of Jesus are being taught to the masses. First of all, oneness means that we are all a part of the whole, no one is separate, no one is greater, we all just are, with the same potential at understanding, the same potential at working miracles, and the same potential at allowing God's power, your power, to move mountains, even if they are just mountains like the mountains of anger in your heart. I myself believe that he was talking about the physical peaks. Next, oneness makes us all the caretakers of the world and the universe if we all are a part and connected to one another and everything in and around us. Think about it. It is said that we come from the Earth and will return to the Earth. Well, so does everything else. Once we drop our bodies, we came from spirit and we return to spirit. We are only different from God the Source in quantity, not quality. Do you get it? Just as the sap of the Pine tree contains the full essence of the entire tree, so do you contain the full essence of God. You are not separate; you are a piece and parcel of the whole. So what keeps you from exhibiting this fact? It is the mind, the misunderstandings, the false teachings, it is everything that we have within us that is clouding, masking our LOVE, the Unconditional Love of God, and that keeps it from flowing freely through us, making itself known to us and everything around us through physical experience. Oneness is an actual spiritual place that can be achieved with deep focus, and perseverance. This state of being has been accomplished by many. This fact is your journey. This fact is the "Seeking of the Kingdom" first, and in your approach, you unify your will with God the Source. You begin to look like God the Source from the inside out, and because of this, all that you seek to experience in this physical life becomes yours as a byproduct of your approach to the Kingdom. The grandest of this is that by seeking the Kingdom first, your accomplishments and successes will lack the pain and suffering that so many experience when their focus is on the gaining of material things versus spiritual growth and allowing the Kingdom and God the Source to become the driving force, the passenger, the friend, the counselor in your life and in all that you do. At the deepest lowest level, you are a direct emanation of God the Source, and as long as you push against this, do not believe this, choose to hold onto misguided and mistaken teachings, you are separate from your true potential, but as soon as you accept this as possibly being true, you begin to see changes in your life and experience because now, for the first time, you have stepped onto the path of "Personal Responsibility", and allowed God to speak and work through you.

Summary:

The point is this: you have been the key all along, and if you deny this or stand in disbelief, you will never achieve any measure of success without it being tied to pain and suffering. The magic or lack thereof is in the doing of Jesus' teaching, thanking him for his blessing of providing a clear path to reconnecting to God the Source, that our Will aligned with God's Will, aligned with our Will, because now it is God's Will as well, be manifest. You are responsible for the return to God. You are responsible for doing the work, having the faith, beginning with just a little bit, and seeing God working in and through you, because you are now allowing God to do so. Jesus tells the disciples directly that he is not going to do anything for them; he is not going to give them faith. It is their responsibility. So we can stop saying that we are waiting on Jesus, or that Jesus is going to do anything for us. You must invoke the power of God in your life. Your faith is the catalyst. If you do not have any, and choose doubt and worry, prepare yourself to be tossed by the winds and waves, the storms of life. The "Kingdom of God", the "Kingdom of Heaven", is inside you, and you must remove everything that you are not, in order to realize this and allow God inside you. "The works that I do, you will do also, and even more", was spoken by Jesus to his disciples and us, in an attempt to explain that the same God that resided in him and afforded him the power to perform miracles resides in us. He goes on to indicate that the goal of all who believe is perfection, where we appear a direct reflection of God, finally realizing our oneness with all things and God the Source. Tremendous were his "Teachings", unleashing were his "Teachings", direct and unapologetic were his "Teachings". Misguidance and misunderstanding have allowed past and present generations to suffer, but you can now begin the change, you can cause the tide to rise in your family by choosing to see the Truth as it is written and applying it in your life. This is the only way to know. It was never meant for anyone to simply believe. It was meant for you to believe only long enough for you to know, without a shadow of a doubt, through your personal experience, what is true and what is not.

Conclusion

It has been a great experience for me, in studying the life of Christ Jesus as it is chronicled in Matthew, Mark, Luke, and John of the King James Version of the Bible. After the events of the past four years (2006-2010) in my life, to come back to the Bible, which is where it all started for me, and to see scriptures that I have never heard discussed. I have seen that all that I have come to know is true, and because my mind has been opened, I could see what had been written all along.

First, Jesus says it plainly that he is not going to do anything for us. It is our responsibility. The occurrences of our lives, the manner in which we live our lives and how we respond to the events that happen in our lives, are all our responsibility.

Jesus never set himself up to be worshipped and/or to have followers. Jesus said that if we follow "His Teachings", we are his friends for he has given us everything that God has given him. He set no rituals in place and no traditions. He spoke of a "Change In Focus", and "A Way of Life", and what a little bit of faith in God could do.

Jesus told us that there is a goal, and that it is not to make it into heaven after a life full of pain and sorrow. Jesus spoke of heaven as being attainable now, reachable now, and through many parables described its location as being deep inside each and every one of us, in the secret chambers, and that if we allow the words of God to germinate and grow from good ground, they will develop into a river of life flowing from the inside out. However, it is up to us to prepare the ground.

Jesus spoke of perfection. Each of us is originally perfect and each of us can work our way back to it, now. Jesus said we cannot be God, but if we are perfect we can be as God, a perfect reflection of it.

Jesus spoke often of the fact that we are all one. He spoke this in reference to children. He spoke this in receiving all manner of individuals, the sick, the healthy, the poor, and the jailed with love and compassion. He also spoke many times of the circle, trying to get each of us to see, without saying it directly. The circle that he spoke of often is that he was in God and God is in him and that if we keep his teachings we are in him and that the same God that is in him is in us. Now if you still do not get this, he is saying that the same God that is in him is in us. This has always been the case. The problem is that man forgets, because he cannot see past his five senses. Jesus tells us over and over, and it all comes together when you look at all that he says in the proper context, and at only what he said.

Jesus says the works that he did we will do also, and even more. How many of you have ever heard this discussed? He was talking to his disciples, you and me. Do you believe it?

There are many things that the masses believe in, say, and do, that are merely rituals and traditions stemming from misunderstanding, that if you truly hold Jesus as the key figure of the biblical scriptures, you will see that he never condoned or even spoke of.

Two commandments were given:
LOVE God with all your heart, soul, and mind, and to LOVE your neighbor as yourself.

That was it. In trying to do so, you will discover all the places in which you need to grow in your approach to being a perfect reflection of God, and the spiritual realization of the oneness of all things.

You are the center of your world, therefore it is your total and complete responsibility either to walk the narrow path as Jesus outlined it, *or not*, to trek the path of the few and not the many, and to align yourself with God the Source of all things that your fruit might be health, wealth, abundance and peace. If you look out in nature, everything works in complete harmony; this includes physical life and death. If you are not seeing this in your life, if you are not in harmony, you may be on the same path as that of the masses. Open your eyes. That is what Jesus would want. That is why he came–not to die–but to open your eyes.

LOVE

About The Author

Being a student of personal development and human potential for 14 years (1997), Benny Ferguson has treaded a path that he wishes on no one. Except that if it is a must, that they emerge from the struggle a Master, a Master Artist ready to begin work on the Master Piece of His Life.

Continuously striving for success in business, and realizing early that the barriers to his personal success lay inside him, was the beginning and the end of a man. With seemingly nowhere to turn for answers, Benny suffered depression, self-sabotage, and paralyzing fear, only to be rewarded in 2005, in the weeks following waking up late one night during a dream, in an angry rage, that mind is the gateway. Within the parallels of science and the major spiritual teachings of the world, reside the truth and a door of Personal Responsibility and Power for each and every human being.

To this day, everything that Benny has discovered about himself, he has discovered is inherent in every human being. There is a way out, and it is universal, because Truth is universal, and it starts with the mind.

- The physical body is only the tip of the iceberg of you and all that you are capable of.
- Your must realize that the physical senses only reveal effects, not causes.
- You must realize that all is inherently GOOD, and to experience less than this is your own doing.
- You must realize that all you desire already exists within you, but the potential to bring it forth is covered by fear and misunderstanding.
- Knowing you, knowing the subtle parts of your being, and knowing the purpose of those faculties sets you free.

There is an Art to succeeding in every area of your life, and every individual human being's Master Piece is different. However, the foundation, the canvas of that Masterpiece is the same; that foundation is understanding. Understanding who you are, on a subconscious, non-physical level, and then mastering the creative faculties that lie within you. These are your art supplies.

LOVE

Connecting With Benny:

Facebook: www.facebook.com/bennyrfergusonjr

Youtube: www.youtube.com/BennyFergusonJr/videos

Twitter: www.twitter.com/BennyRFergusonJ

Contacting Benny:

Initial contacts to Benny for discussions, interviews, one – on - one or group coaching, speaking or training may be made through telephone or email.

Phone: 336-546-7142

Email: BennyFerguson@TheFergusonCompany.com

***Email Benny at BennyFerguson@TheFergusonCompany.com to receive your FREE complimentary "So You Call Yourself A Christian? - Workbook."

Benny Ferguson

www.ingramcontent.com/pod-product-compliance
Lightning Source LLC
LaVergne TN
LVHW021551080426
835510LV00019B/2474